Proverbs and Programs for Women

"A proverb for every problem"

by
WILMA L. SHAFFER

STANDARD PUBLISHING
Cincinnati, Ohio   3107

Library of Congress Catalog Card No. 72-75097

© 1972
The STANDARD PUBLISHING Company
Cincinnati, Ohio
Printed in U.S.A.

Preface

A few years ago when I wrote a devotional book on Psalms, their poetic beauty led us into the temple of God for spiritual uplift. By contrast, the punchy parallelism of Proverbs leads us into the marketplace where the business of living occurs.

The parallelism (lines arranged in pairs) is of thought rather than sound—a balancing of thought against thought, one line an echo of the other. Three kinds appear in Proverbs:

Synonymous—second line repeats the first
example: Proverbs 22:24
Antithetic—second line is a contrast to the first
example: Proverbs 15:32
Synthetic—second line further develops the thought
example: Proverbs 17:20

"Enigmas" abound—proverbs capable of different interpretations.

In this book, each program is unique in presentation, with brief devotional talks, humorous dialogues, parodies, responsive readings, discussion—a variety of ways to study the proverbs and provide programs that are daringly different. Humor gives the necessary light touch for the barbed metaphors, as three wives from King Solomon's harem participate in dialogues:

Naamah—the long-time wife
Persis—from Persia
Shiphrah—from Egypt

I hope you enjoy the wives, wealth, and wisdom from the Golden Age of Israel.

—THE AUTHOR

Contents

CHAPTER I

When You Know Too Much

**"Trust in the Lord with all thine heart;
and lean not unto thine own understanding"
Proverbs 3:5**

THEME SONG: "Some Day He'll Make It Plain"

SCRIPTURE READING: Proverbs 8:1-14

PRAYER: Almighty God, great in majesty and infinite in power, we thank Thee for Thy great love. We see Thy wisdom in the universe, and Thy knowledge in the wonders of creation. When we consider all this, and that we also are the work of Thy hands, we bow in humble gratitude. We seek forgiveness of our sins through Thy Son Jesus, in whose name we pray. Amen.

Preparation: Arrange a display of books. One area of the table will feature such books as texts on astronomy, biology, philosophy, psychology, and child care. The Bible should be in a "featured place," spotlighted, possibly in a central position, surrounded by the knowledge books. Or, the textbooks can be heaped up at one side on the interest table, and the Bible at the other side, with "wisdom" ribbons streaming from the Bible to each book—denoting the source of all wisdom.

7

Wisdom Comes From God

The best educated people of any age live in the world today. Women have more opportunity for education and the resulting freedom than ever before in history. Colleges are bulging with students, even grandparents are going to school! Evening classes are filled quickly, as they present topics ranging from photography to philosophy.

With all this book learning, the world should be filled with wise people. An educated people should be happy people too, shouldn't they? Parents are so full of knowledge and methods on child nurture, this should be an exceptional generation of youngsters, shouldn't it?

Even though the world knows so much, does this guarantee peace and joy for all? Of course it doesn't! When you know too much about *any* subject, your responsibility is greater, your concerns are heavier, your freedom, oddly enough, is curtailed. Why? You are "informed"—you can't excuse yourself by pleading ignorance. You are obligated to become involved. There goes freedom—your peace of mind!

No, this isn't a defense of ignorance, but it is a reminder that with "enlightenment some of the enchantment" may disappear. Also along with the education process must come wisdom, and wisdom is from God. Education should include the knowledge of what to do with it!

> Incline thine ear unto wisdom,
> and apply thine heart to understanding. . . .
> Give instruction to a wise man,
> and he will be yet wiser.
> —*Proverbs 2:2; 9:9*

The language of Proverbs 2:3-11 is beautiful as the thirst for wisdom is compared to silver and hidden treasures. If only you will cry for knowledge and lift up your voice to wisdom, "Then shalt thou understand the fear of the Lord, and find the knowledge of God. For the Lord giveth wisdom: out of his mouth cometh knowledge and understanding. . . . When wisdom entereth into thine heart, and knowledge is pleasant unto thy soul; discretion shall preserve thee, understanding shall keep thee."

Proverbs are as practical as the Psalms are prayerful. Proverbs apply to everyday situations, contrasting wisdom and folly, virtue and vice. As we study the Proverbs you will see that wisdom promises life and says little about enjoyment. Folly promises enjoyment and keeps silent about death. Oh, how the folly of the world confounds its wisdom!

> Unlearned, he knew no schoolman's subtle art,
> No language, but the language of the heart.
> By nature honest, by experience wise,
> Healthy by temperance, and by exercise.
> —*Alexander Pope*

Proverbs present a common sense approach to many of the relationships of life: "to give subtilty to the simple, to the young man knowledge and discretion" (Proverbs 1:4). "Common sense, in an uncommon degree, is what the world calls wisdom" (Coleridge). As a child we learn the facts about God and His universe (knowledge). As an adult, with an understanding heart, we grow in wisdom and deeper understanding of His ways.

"Wisdom is better than rubies" (Proverbs 8:11). "The fear of the Lord is the beginning of wisdom: and the knowledge of the holy is understanding" (Proverbs 9:10).

"The fear of the Lord" involves learning about these three R's: reverence, recognition, revelation. Without reverence you can acquire worldly knowledge far removed from truth. You can labor in the garden of life not recognizing the difference between a weed and a flower. Only when you have reverence for God and His ways can you enter into the realm of the second R: recognition. Purpose and design in all of the universe, as well as in the pattern of daily living, are of God.

Recognition of God's part in the design leads to true wisdom. This acceptance then brings us to acknowledge Him as God—the revealed ONE. Since "It is the glory of God to conceal" (Proverbs 25:2), as well as reveal, your knowledge becomes wisdom when you learn the facts pertinent to your relationship with Him.

We bow before Him and love Him because He first loved us. This devout attitude demonstrates all three of the R's.

Womanly Wisdom

Someone has said that in a conversation no talker should speak more than two or three sentences without pausing for others to say a word. Each one may have much to report, but don't you agree, it is more pleasant if all have a chance to participate—to contribute their ideas to a discussion?

Yes, that may be good advice, but how difficult to abide by it! All of us know talkative women, and most of us take our turns monopolizing conversations. Good conversation is like a Ping-Pong game—each player must return the ball to keep the game going.

Consider these pertinent proverbs: "A fool uttereth all his mind: but a wise man keepeth it in till afterwards" (Proverbs 29:11). "Even a fool, when he holdeth his peace, is counted wise: and he that shutteth his lips is esteemed a man of understanding" (Proverbs 17:28). Or, "Answer not a fool according to his folly, lest thou also be like unto him. . . . Seest thou a man wise in his own conceit? there is more hope of a fool than of him" (Proverbs 26:4, 12). (*These shrewd statements should stimulate a lively discussion. Don't just quote them—talk about them.*)

How dangerous it is to think we have all the answers, but it is also foolish to think we know nothing! Knowledge of God is not like fruit on a tree, waiting to be plucked by the casual passerby. Devotion is required to attain knowledge of God. On your knees, bowing in adoration, reading His Word in reverence, seeking His kingdom in earnest—these attitudes will lead you toward the winsome wisdom of God. Such devotion will lead the seeker away from evil and toward eternal life.

How shall we acquire wisdom? Start with what we have: the voice lifted in inquiry, the ear inclined to hear, the heart applied to understanding, the eye opened to seeing, the hand extended to receiving. "The hearing ear, and the seeing eye, the Lord hath made even both of them" (Proverbs 20:12). "Bow down thine ear, and hear the words of the wise, and apply thine heart unto my knowledge" (Proverbs 22:17).

"Wisdom hath builded her house, she hath hewn out her seven pillars" (Proverbs 9:1). This is a parable similar to the great feast (Luke 14:15-24) in the New Testament. The number seven indicates completeness and perfection. The house may be the church. A banquet is prepared, the invitation is given, all are invited to Wisdom Hall. "Come, eat of my bread, and drink of the wine which I have mingled" (Proverbs 9:5).

> Celestial wisdom calms the mind,
> Providing insight for the spiritually blind.

"A foolish woman is clamorous: she is simple, and knoweth nothing" (Proverbs 9:13). Here is the contrast of wisdom versus folly. "The simple inherit folly: but the prudent are crowned with knowledge" (Proverbs 14:18; also read verse 24). The foolish woman represents the indulgent life. She imitates the call of wisdom as she says, "Stolen waters are sweet, and bread eaten in secret is pleasant" (Proverbs 9:17). She is calling "passengers" to choose the pathway that leads to degradation and death.

What a jewel is the woman whose influence guides others toward appreciation of holy life and obedience to God! What a Jezebel is the woman who uses her influence in the guise of pleasure, to lead people away from divine joy in the presence of God, to a false, temporal joy in earthly things. What a marvelous blessing when a woman has a gentle, soothing voice—and this can be cultivated. The voice of the foolish is described as "clamorous"—how easy it is to develop a whining, complaining tone of voice! What an influence is the quiet, soft voice of a woman whose life is devoted to obeying the heavenly Father!

How wonderful is the winsome wisdom of a woman who dedicates her life to the Lord!

What Do You Really Know?

We see only a little of the ocean,
  A few miles distance from the rocky shore;
But, oh, out there beyond the eye's horizon
  There's more—there's more!

We know only a little of God's love,
  A few rich treasures from His mighty store;
But, oh, out there beyond our life's horizon
  There's more—there's more!

—Adapted

Quotes for Discussion

1. "It is never wise to argue with a fool. Bystanders don't know which is which." Consider Proverbs 26:4, 5.
2. "It is the province of knowledge to speak and the privilege of wisdom to listen" (Oliver Wendell Holmes). Consider Proverbs 17:28.
3. "He's a fool that cannot conceal his wisdom" (Benjamin Franklin). Consider Proverbs 25:2.
4. "Knowledge comes, but wisdom lingers" (Alfred Tennyson). Consider Proverbs 3:19, 20; 24:3-6.
5. "Wisdom is ofttimes nearer when we stoop than when we soar" (William Wordsworth).
6. "A man should never be ashamed to say he has been in the wrong, which is but saying in other words that he is wiser today than he was yesterday" (Alexander Pope).
7. "Where shall wisdom be found?" Read Job 28:12-18, 20, 23, 24, 28.
8. Is education sometimes a disruptive influence? If so, does this mean "ignorance is bliss"? Does more education make the Christian life easier?

CHAPTER II

When You Work Too Hard

**"In all labour there is profit:
but the talk of the lips tendeth only to penury"
Proverbs 14:23**

THEME SONG: "A Place for Every Worker"

SCRIPTURE READING: Proverbs 6:6-11

PRAYER: Our heavenly Father, we thank Thee for the privilege of work. We ask that Thy strength will continue to sustain us during our days in this world. Help us to perform each task willingly and graciously, to Thy glory. Guide us in our priorities, so that our daily work will include the privilege of serving Thee. In Jesus' name we pray. Amen.

Preparation: Print Proverbs 14:23 on a large poster and paste colorful pictures (from magazines) of women working at home, office, or church, around the "proverb of the day." Prepare the discussion quotes for distribution by typing them on small sheets of paper, the edges cut out with pinking shears. Assign these before the meeting, and have a panel of experts to lead the group discussion. Select other appropriate Scriptures, using a concordance.

Work Is God's Way

When household chores or office routine press in upon you, do you ever think, "If only I didn't have so much to do!" In fact you may have wondered why you have to work at all!

Work is God's way since the time of creation. Think of His infinite labor while creating everything, from the largest star in the universe to the smallest insect. Jesus said, "My Father worketh hitherto, and I work" (John 5:17). God is still working in our world, upholding, guiding, sustaining, and by His Spirit, helping mankind to find the better way of life. Did you ever consider the compliment Paul paid all Christians when he wrote, "We . . . [are] workers together with him [God]" (2 Corinthians 6:1)?

Work appeared to be a punishment when first meted out to Adam and Eve after their disobedience, but God is wise in His punishments as well as in His blessings. He also provided a day of rest, and "rest is the sweet sauce of labor" (Plutarch).

(*Read Proverbs* 6:6-11.) The proverbial illustration of the ants is God's way of describing cooperation and industry. Each little ant does its share, carries its load, drags heavy burdens, and prepares for winter during warm summer days. "Light is the task where many share the toil" (Greek poet Homer). Ants also work without an overseer or ruler. You may think, that's OK for ants, they are created that way, but such devotion to work takes real discipline in my life!

Yes, that pesky little ant that we chase out of our picnic baskets, is an example of industrious wisdom, and we are to look at his busyness and learn to be wise. Remember, too, that "God gives every bird its food, but He doesn't throw it into the nest" (J. G. Holland).

"Yet a little sleep, a little slumber, a little folding of the hands to sleep" (Proverbs 6:10)—what a wonderful thought when tiredness fills your body—that's the proverb to enjoy! Then you read the parallel thoughts and learn that the wise man is talking about the sluggard, the lazy person, whom poverty is sure to overcome because he sleeps instead of works. (*Read Proverbs* 21:25, 26.)

The sluggard also uses excuses. He cannot plow because it is too cold, "therefore shall he beg in harvest, and have nothing" (Proverbs 20:4). By way of contrast, "Seest thou a man diligent in his business? he shall stand before kings" (Proverbs 22:29); "He that tilleth his land shall have plenty of bread" (Proverbs 28:19).

Human beings have the strength and the potential to be hard workers. Physical laziness leads not only to poverty, but to impairment of health. Lack of exercise? Look what happens when you step on the scales! No work to do? Laziness grows on people. It begins in cobwebs and ends in chains.

Work is God's way and He is wonderfully wise in all His ways!

Work Is Woman's Way

A certain young mother said enviously to her mother whose children were grown-up, "You've got it made, Mom!" The older mother replied somewhat sadly, "Life isn't having it made. It's the struggle of getting it made." Do you agree? Your answer will be according to your circumstances and stage in life.

Frankly, most of us don't like to work! We do it because of economic pressure, or because we are boxed in and have a job to do. It's great to sleep late (occasionally), to have no menial chore awaiting, to say, "I have nothing to do!" Great, isn't it—or is it? Suppose life were just that way for you. No task to do. No one needing you. Just yourself to pamper and please. Would you really be happy?

A certain city woman seems to "have it made." She lives

alone in a plush apartment, has plenty of money, pleasant friends, and no work to do. A maid comes weekly to clean. However, this woman said, "My home is just a place to live, my friends are just someone to see once in a while. No one needs me!"

Novelist Edna Ferber said, "My philosophy lies in work. If my brimstone and hell were to be on this earth, it would be waking in the morning and having no story to think about, nothing to do but make lunch dates. I believe every adult should have to work for the right to live; if not at household chores, then at a job or craft."

Battling with problems, laboring for loved ones, striving for achievement, bring a certain dignity to life and a sense of deep satisfaction. Read Proverbs 24:27-32 and in your mind underscore the words: field, vineyard, thorns, walls. Your "field" may be your home, and your "vineyard" the children that grow there. Unless you combine work with prayer, "thorns and nettles" will cover your abode, and the walls will crumble.

Tender plants require careful attention. Thorns and weeds grow without cultivation or irrigation. A vineyard requires diligent care. While the caretaker sleeps, the elements of nature—wind, water, weeds—do their work.

The stone wall in the spiritual realm could refer to the commands of God. If they are obeyed, they keep out the destructive elements of life. If disobeyed, the protective walls crumble and destructive forces rush into our lives. Woman plays an important part in keeping these walls of faith strong. Work is woman's way of life! To be needed makes her happiest. To do the job well gives her fulfillment.

So, while we grumble and complain about our busy lives, let us remember we are *participating* in life, not just looking on.

How difficult it is to do your work well if you think it is of no importance! How can washing dishes every day really be important? Well, try leaving them stacked in the sink for a week and see how essential that daily chore is! Try leaving the office mail accumulate for a week, or the correspondence filing pile up for a few weeks. Arousing enthusiasm for the details of any job may be difficult, yet there are no rules for success in any job that work, unless you do. It is much easier to do a job right than to explain why you did it wrong, or not at all.

Try this approach for getting a job done:
1. Get started—often the hardest part!
2. Manage your time—don't let it manage you.
3. Set deadlines—and meet them if possible.
4. Concentrate on the relevant—set aside the tasks that can wait awhile.
5. Develop your own tempo—avoid trying to match the pace of a neighbor.
6. Complete the job. Oh yes, there are some jobs, like dishes and diapers, that need doing over again and again; but do each day's work as cheerfully as possible!

"In all labour there is profit: but the talk of the lips tendeth only to penury" (Proverbs 14:23). Ten-year-old Tommy told his grandmother, "I have asked for money, begged for money, cried for money." She asked, "Have you thought of *working* for it?" "Well, it's like this," Tommy said, "I'm going through the alphabet and I haven't got to W yet!" Many people are like Tommy—it is easier to use the "lips" than the hands.

Jesus was not ashamed of working with His hands. The apostle Paul made tents. With the Lord, all honest work is honorable, and all dishonest work, even that of a judge or king, is dishonorable.

Can one be "busy" yet not truly working? A thought-provoking legend tells about "laborious idleness." A wealthy king in the northland, at great cost and servant labor, built an ice palace from slabs of ice from the lake. Dressed in furs and jewels, he sat in splendor during the springtime, and into summer when the palatial palace melted and dissolved into slushy mud. What a waste of money and hard work!

To be lazy in your work is compared to "him that is a great waster" (Proverbs 18:9). The idler does not so much waste time, as he wastes himself. The real dignity of work is found when "He that laboureth laboureth for himself; for his mouth craveth it of him" (Proverbs 16:26). Attitude makes the difference. "A willing heart brightens the work, and gives all tasks, humble and great, the dignity and power required for success." Enjoy the job and it will appear easy and be quickly completed!

Work is woman's way and she is wonderfully efficient in the variety of tasks that make up her day.

Discussion

1. Compare Proverbs 6:6 with Proverbs 20:4.
2. "Waste not—want not." Is this good advice spiritually as well as economically?
3. Should a Christian retire from work at age sixty-five?
4. "A servant works—a king speaks." Read Proverbs 22:29. (See Chapter X for a fuller discussion of leadership.)
5. "People work better under the attitude of approval than the atmosphere of criticism." Do you agree?
6. "No race can prosper till it learns that there is as much dignity in tilling a field as in writing a poem" (Booker T. Washington).
7. "Do life's plain, common work as it comes, certain that daily duties and daily bread are the sweetest things of life" (Robert Louis Stevenson).

Two Women at Work

Two women in the office
  Typed from day to day.
Both did the same kind of labor,
  Both received the same small pay.
One heart was heavy and sad,
  One heart was always gay;
One worked with many a sigh,
  One smiled all the day.

Two mothers in their homes
  Cared for children day by day.
Both had the same kind of labor,
  Both had the same kind of pay.
One heart was heavy and sad,
  One heart was always gay;
One worked with many a sigh,
  One smiled all the day.

—Adapted

CHAPTER III

When You Spend Too Much

**"Riches certainly make themselves wings;
they fly away as an eagle toward heaven"
Proverbs 23:5**

THEME SONG: "Ivory Palaces"

SCRIPTURE READING: Proverbs 3:9-18

PRAYER: Father in heaven, we praise Thee for Thy goodness to us. May we use the material blessings to honor Thee, as well as to care for our own daily needs. Give us wisdom in placing Thy way first in our lives. Help us to walk humbly and gratefully with Thee each day as our guide. In Jesus' name we pray. Amen.

Preparation: Have a "money" exhibit. Let the coin collectors bring a display and speak briefly about their hobby. Arrange a money tree, then present it as a gift to your benevolent project of the month. Make a poster showing current economic trends, or the value of the dollar, and how much (or little) it will buy. Print this statement on a bulletin board or a poster: "Money talks—but nowadays a $ doesn't have enough ¢ to say much."

23

Budget Bound

I don't suppose King Solomon worried much about money. His annual income was 666 talents of gold, or $20,000,000. One gift from the Queen of Sheba amounted to $3,500,000. His shields were of gold; all the vessels of his palace were gold, and his throne was ivory overlaid with gold. Besides this, he had to support 700 wives and 300 concubines in expensive splendor!

Luxury, wealth, and the wooing of these pagan women eventually led wise King Solomon away from God. Could we say he "spent too much"?

This wealthy king knew that "wisdom is better than rubies" (Proverbs 8:11), yet he accumulated rubies and other precious gems. He knew that a man "becometh poor that dealeth with a slack hand: but the hand of the diligent maketh rich" (Proverbs 10:4), yet his diligence became "slack" as he grew older. He knew "He that gathereth in summer is a wise son: but he that sleepeth in harvest is a son that causeth shame" (Proverbs 10:5), yet in the harvest years this king turned away from God. He knew "He that trusteth in his riches shall fall: but the righteous shall flourish as a branch" (Proverbs 11:28), yet he neglected the spiritual side of his life. This seems to be the weakness of our human nature.

Most homemakers, rather than having King Solomon's problem of too much wealth, are more concerned about keeping within the budget! The family grows, clothes shrink, the budget grows, income shrinks. But if love is present, there is no need for wealth! "Better is a dinner of herbs where love is, than a stalled ox and hatred therewith" (Proverbs 15:17).

This proverb also is comforting to the budget-bound homemaker: "The ransom of a man's life are his riches: but the poor heareth not rebuke" (Proverbs 13:8). "Wealth gotten by vanity shall be diminished: but he that gathereth by labour shall increase" (Proverbs 13:11). Vanity means by chance, or good luck, or inheritance. A modern proverb would be "Easy come, easy go."

Abraham Lincoln did not admire mere financial success. He once said, "Financial success is purely metallic. The man who gains it has four attributes: gold in his palm, silver on his tongue, brass in his face, and iron in his heart." What a sharp commentary on the priorities of the wealthy!

An old-fashioned word seems to be lost from our economic vocabulary—thrift. This word means making the best use of what you have, and enjoying it more. Or, as Phyllis McGinley wrote in *Sixpence in Her Shoe*: "When thrift serves stew to the family to ease the budget, it sees to it that the dish is savory as *filet mignon*; and it delights to share with anyone who comes to the door."*

Proverbs 22:9 expresses thrift plus generosity: "He that hath a bountiful eye shall be blessed; for he giveth of his bread to the poor." Who are the poor? Proverbs refer to needy or poor with at least four meanings:

1. An uninfluential person, not necessarily destitute.
2. The needy person, actually in want through bereavement, infirmity, or a calamity that deprives him of the necessities of life.
3. The sad and afflicted person who has a patient and humble dependence on God.
4. The destitute person.

Often the proverbial reference to the poor means that large segment of people who have no margin of security if financial problems arise.

Rich or poor financially, you can find yourself "poor" according to one of these categories!

How long has it been since you heard someone say, "I can't afford it!" It takes willpower to use this valuable phrase when all your friends appear to be members of the affluent

---

*© 1960, 1962, 1963, 1964 by Phyllis McGinley. Published by The MacMillan Company. Used by permission.

society. Everyone, even governments, could profit by applying this commonsensical approach to economics: we can't afford it.

Try sorting out want or selfish desire from real needs. This concept can be applied to more areas of life than money problems. Decide the demands on your time and energy by asking the questions, "Is it worth it?" and "Can I afford it?" In the Sermon on the Mount Jesus spoke about treasures: "Lay not up for yourselves treasures upon earth, where moth and rust doth corrupt, and where thieves break through and steal: but lay up for yourselves treasures in heaven, where neither moth nor rust doth corrupt, and where thieves do not break through nor steal: for where your treasure is, there will your heart be also" (Matthew 6:19-21).

Responsive Reading

SHOPPERS' LAMENT

LEADER: When I spend too much the bills pile high,
      But I have lots of friends standing by.
RESPONSE: Wealth maketh many friends; but the poor is separated from his neighbour (Proverbs 19:4).
ALL: He that trusteth in his riches shall fall (Proverbs 11:28).

LEADER: When I spend too much then folks will see
      That I'm not as wise as I ought to be.
RESPONSE: Poverty and shame shall be to him that refuseth instruction: but he that regardeth reproof shall be honoured (Proverbs 13:18).
ALL: He that trusteth in his riches shall fall.

LEADER: When I spend too much who should care?
      It's my inheritance and there's cash to spare!

RESPONSE: An inheritance may be gotten hastily at the beginning; but the end thereof shall not be blessed (Proverbs 20:21).

ALL: He that trusteth in his riches shall fall.

LEADER: Money talks, I will agree;
All it says is good-bye to me.

RESPONSE: Riches certainly make themselves wings; they fly away as an angel toward heaven (Proverbs 23:5).

ALL: He that trusteth in his riches shall fall.

LEADER: I spend a fortune at the grocery store,
Two days later, return for more.

RESPONSE: Much food is in the tillage of the poor: but there is that is destroyed for want of judgment (Proverbs 13:23).

ALL: He that trusteth in his riches shall fall.

LEADER: When I spend too much I am money mad,
Then a guilty feeling leaves me sad.

RESPONSE: The rich man's wealth is his strong city, and as an high wall in his own conceit (Proverbs 18:11).

ALL: He that trusteth in his riches shall fall.

LEADER: When I spend too much for jewels and rings,
Too late I discover they are useless things.

RESPONSE: There is gold, and a multitude of rubies: but the lips of knowledge are a precious jewel (Proverbs 20:15).

ALL: He that trusteth in his riches shall fall.

LEADER: When I spend too much, I go from rich to poor.
Why am I so foolish? Well, I'm not sure!

RESPONSE: The rich and poor meet together: the Lord is the maker of them all (Proverbs 22:2).

ALL: He that trusteth in his riches shall fall.

LEADER: When I spend too much, more money I borrow,
   Then I plunge in deeper to financial sorrow.
RESPONSE: The rich ruleth over the poor, and the borrower
   is servant to the lender (Proverbs 22:7).
ALL: He that trusteth in his riches shall fall.

LEADER: When I spend too much to help another,
   I'll benefit too, as well as my brother.
RESPONSE: He that hath pity upon the poor lendeth unto the
   Lord; and that which he hath given will he pay him again
   (Proverbs 19:17).
ALL: He that trusteth in his riches shall fall.

Discussion

1. "Labour not to be rich: cease from thine own wisdom" (Proverbs 23:4). Consider three aspects of wealth: The substantial good, the transitory or fleeting quality, and unworthy as a goal.
2. "A fool and his money are welcome everywhere." Compare with Proverbs 19:4. Remember to define "poor."
3. Discuss reasons for the pretense of Proverbs 13:7.
4. Can life become too easy? Alexander Pope expressed it this way: "Stretched on the rack of a too easy chair." Discuss.
5. "Prosperity tries the fortunate: adversity the great," said Pliny the Younger, Roman scholar. Consider Proverbs 14:20; 18:16.

Treasures

Out of this life I shall never take
Things of silver and gold I make.
All that I cherish and hoard away
After I leave, on this earth must stay.
Though I have toiled for a painting rare
To hang on the wall, I must leave it there.
Though I call it mine, and boast its worth,
I must give it up when I leave this earth.
All that I gather, and all that I keep
I must leave behind when I fall asleep.

And I often wonder what I shall own
In that other life, when I pass alone.
What shall they find, and what
Shall they see, in the soul that
Answers the call for me?
Shall the Great Judge learn
When my task is through,
That my spirit has gathered some riches too?
Or shall at last it be mine to find
That all I'd worked for I'd left behind.

CHAPTER IV

When Your Tongue Is Careless

"A wholesome tongue is a tree of life"
Proverbs 15:4

THEME SONG: "Wonderful Words of Life"

SCRIPTURE READING: Proverbs 12:17-23

PRAYER: Father in heaven, we thank Thee for the gift of speech. Help us to say the right words in the right way, every day of our lives. Make us aware of the power of the tongue for evil or good. May we use our vocabulary to praise Thy name and present Thy Word to others. In Jesus' name. Amen.

Special Feature: From newspapers or church magazines, cut out several photos of famous people who are "speaking." Paste the pictures on pieces of construction paper, and assign a number to each. Give a prize to the person who identifies the most speakers. To make the contest more difficult, use only the lower half of the faces. Let the contestants identify the speakers by their nose and mouth only.

Tree of Life

Probably you have considered many descriptions of your tongue, but have you ever thought of it as a "tree of life," bearing fruit according to the words that flow from it? This is one of the beautiful metaphors from Proverbs regarding that "little member," the tongue (read Proverbs 15:4 and James 3:1-11). How important is the tongue?

"Death and life are in the power of the tongue: and they that love it shall eat the fruit thereof" (Proverbs 18:21). What a powerful part of our body is the tongue! Sometimes when we use our tongues carelessly, it is to tell a friend what someone else has said about her. If the words wound our friend, we have done two things: placed the person we are quoting in a difficult relationship, and hurt the one we are telling.

Talebearing often masquerades as concern for the person: "I thought you would want to know." Actually the damaging revelation is made because of a secret desire to wound. We don't even recognize this tendency in ourselves. It is childish, of course!

Notice the self-righteous pride in little faces as children "tell on each other." When adults carry the glad tidings of someone's naughtiness, they are acting like children.

What control the tongue requires! How ashamed and sad we are when harmful words have been uttered! On the other hand, when you have spoken wisely, using just the right words, this proverb will apply: "A word fitly spoken is like apples of gold in pictures of silver" (Proverbs 25:11). "A man hath joy by the answer of his mouth: and a word spoken in due season, how good is it!" (Proverbs 15:23).

When you respond calmly in a tense situation: "Pleasant words are as an honeycomb, sweet to the soul, and health to the bones" (Proverbs 16:24). Words can change the currents of life. Sharp words pierce to the bone. "A soft answer turneth away wrath: but grievous words stir up anger" (Proverbs 15:1).

How much of ourselves is revealed through the movement of our tongues! "A fool's lips enter into contention . . . A fool's mouth is his destruction, and his lips are the snare of his soul" (Proverbs 18:6, 7). Sometimes when we speak, we reveal the spiritual barrenness of our souls. "The mouth of a righteous man is a well of life: but violence covereth the mouth of the wicked. . . . In the lips of him that hath understanding wisdom is found" (Proverbs 10:11, 13). Careful choice of words or significant silence reveal our wisdom or foolishness.

"He that hath knowledge spareth his words . . . Even a fool, when he holdeth his peace, is counted wise" (Proverbs 17:27, 28). "The lips of the righteous feed many: but fools die for want of wisdom" (Proverbs 10:21).

When the tongue is controlled, "The words . . . are as deep waters, and the wellspring of wisdom as a flowing brook" (Proverbs 18:4) and thus a blessing for all the ears that heed the words. When the tongue is carelessly used, profanity, falsehood, flattery, and slander result. "He that goeth about as a talebearer revealeth secrets: therefore meddle not with him that flattereth with his lips" (Proverbs 20:19). "A false witness shall not be unpunished, and he that speaketh lies shall not escape" (Proverbs 19:5). "He that hideth hatred with lying lips, and he that uttereth a slander, is a fool. . . . He that refraineth his lips is wise" (Proverbs 10:18, 19).

> A careless tongue may kindle strife.
> A cruel tongue may wreck a life.
> A brutal tongue may smite and kill.
> A tattling tongue may warp the will.
> A gracious tongue will smooth the way.
> A joyous tongue will light the day.
> A timely tongue will lessen stress.
> A loving tongue will heal and bless.
> —*Author Unknown*

Thoughts come and go spontaneously, but well-ordered speech is the gift of God.

Bible Times Dialogue

This dialogue introduces two fictitious characters from the harem of King Solomon. In this episode two wives discuss the arrival of a new wife, using proverbial responses. Women in your group will enjoy the variety of presenting proverbs in this dramatic way. The harem wives may wear costumes and memorize their roles, if you wish. Or the speeches may be read responsively, with only a brief rehearsal to allow the cast to become acquainted with the material so that they can use dramatic pause and expression.

HAREM HOUSEHOLD

Setting: Royal House of the Women
Cast: Naamah and Persis
(Two wives of King Solomon)

NAAMAH: My husband, the king, has taken a new wife.

PERSIS: Our husband, the king, has added a "strange woman" to his harem, and her lips "drop as an honeycomb, and her mouth is smoother than oil" (Proverbs 5:3).

NAAMAH: Beware, Persis, lest you become "snared with the words of thy mouth" (Proverbs 6:2). My husband, the king, says: "He that answereth a matter before he heareth it, it is folly and shame unto him" (Proverbs 18:13). You haven't met Shiphrah yet. Another wife offended is "harder to be won than a strong city: and [her] contentions are like the bars of a castle" (Proverbs 18:19). This applies especially to new wives!

PERSIS (*laughing*): "Even in laughter the heart is sorrowful; and the end of that mirth is heaviness" (Proverbs 14:13).

NAAMAH (*soothingly*): Cheer up. "Heaviness in the heart . . .
maketh it stoop: but a good word maketh it glad" (Proverbs 12:25).

PERSIS: "A word spoken in due season, how good is it!" (Proverbs 15:23). Yes, Naamah, "Pleasant words are as an
honeycomb, sweet to the soul, and health to the bones"
(Proverbs 16:24).

NAAMAH: Yea, my husband, the king, says, "Whoso loveth
instruction loveth knowledge: but he that hateth reproof
is brutish" (Proverbs 12:1). "Hear; for I will speak of
excellent things; and the opening of my lips shall be
right things" (Proverbs 8:6). He is a wise man!

PERSIS: Wise in many ways, but not in the way of a woman!
Yesterday when I told Puah about the new wife, she wept.
Some of us are angry, not sad.

NAAMAH: "The words of a talebearer are as wounds" (Proverbs 18:8). My husband says, "He that goeth about as a
talebearer revealeth secrets: therefore meddle not with
him that flattereth with his lips" (Proverbs 20:19).

PERSIS: You know his words well, Naamah. You have lived
here a long time. "The tongue of the just is as choice silver:
the heart of the wicked is little worth" (Proverbs 10:20).
The new wife has a wicked heart, I've heard.

NAAMAH: "The wicked is snared by the transgression of his
lips" (Proverbs 12:13). How true that "In the mouth of
the foolish is a rod of pride: but the lips of the wise shall
preserve them" (Proverbs 14:3).

PERSIS: She is certainly proud! Have you seen her—those
fabulous jewels—the painted eyes—the way she walks!

NAAMAH (*sighing*): I have seen her. Shiphrah is her name
and it means splendor. It is a comfort to know: "Every
one that is proud in heart is an abomination to the Lord"
(Proverbs 16:5).

PERSIS: "The getting of treasures by a lying tongue is a vanity tossed to and fro of them that seek death" (Proverbs 21: 6). "Wealth gotten by vanity shall be diminished" (Proverbs 13:11).

NAAMAH: Vanity! Vanity! That is the way of our life here! "He that is greedy of gain troubleth his own house" (Proverbs 15:27). I am accustomed to sharing my husband, the king. "All the ways of a man are clean in his own eyes; but the Lord weigheth the spirits" (Proverbs 16:2).

PERSIS: "In the light of the king's countenance is life; and his favour is as a cloud of the latter rain" (Proverbs 16: 15).

NAAMAH: Yea, we covet his favor! "Righteous lips are the delight of kings" (Proverbs 16:13). "The wise in heart shall be called prudent: and the sweetness of the lips increaseth learning" (Proverbs 16:21).

PERSIS: If only our husband, the king, would drink water from his own cistern, and running water from his own well (Proverbs 5:15)! "Can a man take fire in his bosom, and his clothes not be burned? Can one go upon hot coals, and his feet not be burned?" (Proverbs 6:27, 28).

NAAMAH: "He that diligently seeketh good procureth favour: but he that seeketh mischief, it shall come unto him" (Proverbs 11:27).

PERSIS: "He that troubleth his own house shall inherit the wind: and the fool shall be servant to the wise of heart" (Proverbs 11:29). Soon we meet the proud Shiphrah, and we shall see what happens!

The Tongue

The boneless tongue so small and weak
Can crush and kill, declared the Greek.
The tongue destroys a greater horde,
The Turk asserts, than does the sword.

The Persian proverb wisely saith,
A lengthy tongue, an early death.
Or sometimes takes this form instead,
Don't let your tongue cut off your head.

The tongue can speak a word whose speed,
Says the Chinese, outstrips the steed.
While Arab sages this impart,
The tongue's great storehouse is the heart.

From Hebrew writers this maxim has sprung,
Though feet may slip, ne'er let the tongue.
The sacred writer crowns the whole,
Who keeps his tongue, doth keep his soul.

—*Author Unknown*

CHAPTER V

When You Feel Trapped

"The fear of man bringeth a snare:
but whoso putteth his trust in the Lord shall be safe"
Proverbs 29:25

THEME SONG: "Safe Am I"

SCRIPTURE READING: Proverbs 1:20-33; 29:25

PRAYER: Heavenly Father, we come to Thee as children who love Thee and need assurance of Thy protective care. Often we are fearful of the problems that surround us. We try to solve them without Thy wisdom. Keep us out of the traps we make for ourselves. Help us to look up to Thee and to rely on Thy great strength. In Jesus' name. Amen.

Special Feature: Have a Birthday Buffet, with cakes decorated for specific months, using twelve cakes if your group is large enough. For smaller groups, combine months by the quarter, using four cakes. Serve coffee or tea, mints and nuts. Plan some special birthday recognitions.

Trapped by Circumstance

What do the Proverbs say about freedom? Did people in the days of King Solomon ever have "trapped" feelings, the frustration of being "caught in a cage"? Was the king with all his wealth and power really a captive of his position? Were the bartered and beautiful wives in the harem prisoners of the circumstances and the historical times? One of the ways life traps people is through circumstances, sometimes beyond their control.

The book of Proverbs is filled with warnings on how to avoid (and control) circumstances that lead to evil. (Other chapters in this book have discussed specific problems.) Youth are warned to listen to the instruction of their parents and to wear the law like "an ornament of grace unto thy head, and chains about thy neck" (Proverbs 1:9).

The common cry of youth is "You don't understand." Each generation inherits a different set of circumstances, possibly a faster pace of life, and must learn to live with it and adjust to it. However, the personal problems of commitment to God are as old as Solomon and as new as tomorrow's baby.

We live in an age that thinks being lost in the woods is a new freedom. Written in the early 1800's, a beautiful allegory from Nathaniel Hawthorne's pen, "Young Goodman Brown," describes a young man lost in the woods of life. He has left Faith behind—Faith is the name of his wife. What effective symbolism there is in the names used for both characters!

The Proverbs refer to the loneliness of such a woodsy adventure: "As a bird that wandereth from her nest, so is a man that wandereth from his place" (Proverbs 27:8). Proverbs also refer to "the goodman is not at home, he is gone a long journey: he hath taken a bag of money with him, and will come home at the day appointed" (Proverbs 7:19, 20).

The young husband cannot rid himself of his obligation to life any easier than the wife and mother. Either one may feel "trapped" or gloriously free in the home situation; it is a matter of attitude—spelled LOVE.

"False freedom leaves a man free to do what he likes; true freedom, to do what he ought."

Freedom, whatever it is, cannot be freedom from obligation. In the New Testament freedom means "release from sin." The truth shall make you free (John 8:32)—free to become children of God. Such freedom is positive, involving obedience, respect, consideration, love. God sent His Son to show us the way out of the woods of darkness and sin.

Most of us claim the good we do as our own ideas, and the evil we do as caused by circumstances beyond our control. Proverbs regards our good deeds as a result of God working in us, when we have surrendered our will to Him.

"For the Lord giveth wisdom: out of his mouth cometh knowledge and understanding. He layeth up sound wisdom for the righteous: he is a buckler to them that walk uprightly" (Proverbs 2:6, 7). (*Also read Proverbs 2:6-17, 20-22.*)

Most of our misfortunes are the result of our own folly. We are too impatient, impetuous, self-willed. "He that hasteth with his feet sinneth. The foolishness of man perverteth his way: and his heart fretteth against the Lord" (Proverbs 19: 2, 3).

What an indication of our foolishness to turn to God only when we fret! How negligent we are to rely on our own brand of goodness rather than on His strength and power! "There are many devices in a man's heart; nevertheless the counsel of the Lord, that shall stand" (Proverbs 19:21).

Fear affects our circumstances: fear of the future, fear of change. We worry about many things that will never happen. Most proverbs are sharp rather than soothing, but this one regarding fear is unique: "When thou liest down, thou shalt not be afraid: yea, thou shalt lie down, and thy sleep shall be sweet" (Proverbs 3:24). Here is another use of fear (awe): "The fear of the Lord prolongeth days: but the years of the wicked shall be shortened" (Proverbs 10:27).

Turn to God's Word for comfort when circumstances seem too much for your peace of mind. Seek His guidance in solving your problems.

Trapped by Age

Most of us not only respect old age, we approach it with extreme caution, taking as much time as possible to arrive.

One Sunday morning when the teacher of a ladies' Sunday-school class asked, "Do birthdays bother you?" the responses were as follows:

"I enjoy my birthdays, thankful for each one!"

"Age doesn't bother me—it is a quality of mind."

"I'm thankful for all the appliances that help me keep young"—she meant dentures, hearing aids, girdles, etc.

"How can I resent growing older? The alternative is death!"

"I like what Victor Hugo said: Forty is the old age of youth; fifty is the youth of old age."

"Birthdays don't bother me in a group of people about the same age. It's when I'm with the young people or children that I feel my age."

"Most birthdays don't bother me—just the ones with zeros!"

Age depends on perspective. A grandmother and her seven-year-old granddaughter were driving through the suburb where the little girl's daddy went to school. When the grandmother mentioned this, the child asked sincerely, "You mean it's still standing?" Where did that place Grandma, age-wise?

Sixteen has always been a magical year, even in a time when privileges are allowed at younger ages. In many states driving a car, for example, is still saved for the sixteen-year-old. This summer, as I write this chapter, eighteen-year-olds have won the right to vote (1971). Yes, birthdays are important, as well as a bother!

The Bible contains so many wonderful stories about the accomplishments of "older" people. Women had babies at age ninety, men set out to conquer worlds at advanced ages. Proverbs tells us, "The glory of young men is their strength:

and the beauty of old men is the gray head" (Proverbs 20:29). And "The hoary head is a crown of glory, if it be found in the way of righteousness" (Proverbs 16:31).

Despite hair tint and the wig fad, gray hair has a peculiar attractiveness. It can be the symbol of wisdom. It should be! Godliness makes the gray-haired person more beautiful.

Somehow in this generation, the emphasis shifted to youth —their importance, their needs, their opportunities. We have been taught to dread the time when children leave home, when the waist thickens, when gray comes into the hair.

The writer of Proverbs succinctly states one of the true joys of growing older is becoming grandparents. "Children's children are the crown of old men; and the glory of children are their fathers" (Proverbs 17:6). Parents rejoice in a virtuous line of descendants, and children eventually are proud of virtuous ancestry.

Let us consider some of the positive reasons for looking forward to the middle years of life.

Uncluttered days. You are free from many of the duties of homemaking, the unending demands of child care, the inevitable involvement in organizations. You can read, take a walk, have a candlelit dinner with your husband or a friend.

Emotionally free. Gone are the petty problems of rearing children and the fears for their safety. Of course you feel concern for grandchildren or neighborhood children, but their problems and safety are their parents' worry.

Maternal pride. You watch the achievements of launched, successful children. Even mistakes in child rearing are in the past, and you can relax.

Better communication with God. You have time to study, and time to pray without so many interruptions.

Remember this: when you begin to notice what a jolly time the young people are having, you're getting old. You may be old at forty and young at eighty; but you are genuinely old at any age if:

You feel old.

You feel you have learned all there is to learn.

You find yourself saying, "I'm too old to do that."

You feel tomorrow holds no promise.

You take no interest in the activities of youth.

You would rather talk than listen.

You long for the good old days, feeling they were best.

The art of living involves the realization that each stage of life is preparation for the next. Each changing scene brings challenge as well as disappointments. The "forward" look of living is one of the secrets of successful aging.

One of the fears of growing older, more than the fear of death, is the dread of being helpless or dependent on others. It is much harder to graciously accept help than to give it. It is more difficult to be still than to be active. Try it some time!

When physical disabilities come, the mind must stay busy. If the mind is affected as age creeps on, loved ones will have to take over and make decisions for the afflicted one.

How effectively one has achieved spiritual maturity will become increasingly evident as the years pass. Have you really given up childish ways? (1 Corinthians 13:11). Do you really have to go through a second childhood? "Let your age be measured by spiritual progress."

Usually the qualities of a personality are intensified as you grow older. If you were cantankerous as a forty-year-old, probably you will be more so at seventy. If you were critical and bitter at forty, probably you will be more so at seventy. Similarly, if you develop a patient, Christlike spirit by forty, your attitude at seventy will have blossomed forth into true maturity.

The fact that more years stretch behind you than ahead should challenge you to rejoice in each day. One of the many marvels of middle age is that you have climbed a mountain—now enjoy the view from the heights!

At every stage of life we are expected to be a certain kind of person. Take pleasure in being a mature person! A good definition of maturity is, "The growing awareness that you are neither quite so wonderful nor quite so hopeless as you once believed. It is making peace between what is and what might be" (Drury).

Discussion

1. Ask several women to share their career/homemaking experiences. The benefit for everyone will be the realization that all positions may lead workers to feel trapped. It all depends on attitude.
2. Can there be freedom apart from God? Consider Proverbs 21:30, 31. Pray for church leadership and for national leadership.
3. Can we be trapped in life by our fears? Consider Proverbs 28:1, 14; 29:25.
4. Discuss the following quotes. Tell which one you like best and why.

> Youth is a blunder; manhood is a struggle;
> old age is a regret.—Disraeli

> The Wine of Life keeps oozing drop by drop,
> the Leaves of Life keep falling one by one.—Fitzgerald

> The measure of a man's life is the well spending of it,
> and not the length.—Plutarch

Mature Love

Lovingly he looks at her
  And sees what she used to be—
Fresh lipped and brown haired,
  Round limbed, graceful as a tree.

Twinkling she smiles at him
  And sees in him the same —
The lover that through the years
  Aroused in her heart a flame.

I admire such a marvelous marriage,
  A couple whose love continues to grow;
And enviously, wonderingly, pray
  That some day such love I'll know.
                              —*W. L. S.*

✦✦✦✦✦✦✦✦

I shall not mind the whiteness of my hair,
Or that slow steps falter on the stair,
Or that young friends hurry as they pass,
Or what strange image greets me in the glass—
If I can feel, as roots feel in the sod,
That I am growing older
  to bloom before the face of God.
                              —*Author Unknown*

CHAPTER VI

When Your Family Needs Guidance

**"A wise son maketh a glad father:
but a foolish son is the heaviness of his mother"
Proverbs 10:1**

THEME SONG: "Happy the Home When God Is There"

SCRIPTURE READING: Proverbs 10:1-12

PRAYER: Father in heaven, we pray that our families on earth will know the same oneness and joy that is known in the heavenly home. Help us to remove from our lives the unworthy things that bring conflict among us. Give us understanding and love. Establish in us a knowledge of right and wrong as found in Thy Word. May each member of our families be dedicated to Jesus, in whose name we pray. Amen.

Preparation: Assign the roles in the dialogue, "The New Wife Arrives." Plan to use buzz groups also, assigning several proverbs on a specific topic to each group. Use current newspaper or magazine articles on family life trends to correlate

47

with the proverbs studies. The "Proverbial Hints for Happy Homes" may be read as a closing devotional. A devotional object talk is also provided with this chapter.

Buzz Groups

Divide those present into five groups, even if the attendance is small in number. Three people can function in a buzz discussion, if your total is fifteen. Assign eight or ten people to a group if the attendance numbers forty or fifty.

Pass out the topics and lists of proverbs, also the related newspaper clippings. Allow the groups ten minutes to discuss the problems and proverbs. Ask each group to appoint someone to report the gist of the discussion. Ten-minute reports from each group will make this an hour-long program. You may wish to shorten this discussion if you use the dialogue and special features, including music.

The five topics and proverbs are as follows:
1. The Importance of Inheritance
   Proverbs 13:22; 17:6; 20:21; 22:28; 23:10-12
2. The Importance of Instruction
   Proverbs 1:2-8; 3:21; 6:20, 21; 13:1; 20:11; 22:6
3. Words for the Wife
   Proverbs 12:4; 14:1; 18:22; 19:13, 14; 27:15; 31:10-31
4. Words for the Husband
   Proverbs 5:18; 16:20; 17:6, 25; 20:7; 23:24-26
5. Cautions for Children
   Proverbs 10:5; 13:1; 19:26-29; 20:20; 22:15; 23:22

Dialogue

The New Wife Arrives

Setting: Court Garden
Cast: Naamah, Persis, Shiphrah

SHIPHRAH: Well, my ladies! I wear the jeweled crown now!

NAAMAH: My husband the king says, "Get wisdom . . . she shall give to thine head an ornament of grace: a crown of glory shall she deliver to thee" (4:7, 9) I never cared much for the jeweled crown; it it too heavy.

PERSIS: Shiphrah wears the jeweled crown, and she sows discord among us. Six things the Lord hates, yea seven: "A proud look, a lying tongue, and hands that shed innocent blood, an heart that deviseth wicked imaginations, feet that be swift in running to mischief, a false witness that speaketh lies" (6:17-19).

SHIPHRAH (*laughing disdainfully*): You are envious, my dear Persis. "I have decked my bed with coverings of tapestry, with carved works, with fine linen of Egypt. I have perfumed my bed with myrrh, aloes, and cinnamon" (7:16, 17).

NAAMAH: What good are tapestry and perfume? "Wisdom hath builded her house, she hath hewn out her seven pillars" (9:1). My husband the king says, "The fear of the Lord is the beginning of wisdom" (9:10).

PERSIS: "Pride goeth before destruction, and an haughty spirit before a fall" (16:18). The new one among us (*glances significantly at Shiphrah*) will not always be the favored one. "The king's wrath is as the roaring of a lion; but his favour is as dew upon the grass" (19:12).

NAAMAH: "House and riches are the inheritance of fathers: and a prudent wife is from the Lord" (19:14). "Most men will proclaim every one his own goodness: but a faithful man who can find?" (20:6)

SHIPHRAH: I expected you old-timers to be jealous! "Who can say, I have made my heart clean, I am pure from my sin?" (20:9). "Even a child is known by his doings, whether his work be pure, and whether it be right" (20:11).

PERSIS: Our husband the king says, "It is better to dwell in a corner of the house top, than with a brawling woman in a wide house" (21:9). Yes, 'tis "better to dwell in the wilderness" (21:19).

NAAMAH: "A good name is rather to be chosen than great riches, and loving favour rather than silver and gold. The rich and poor meet together: the Lord is the maker of them all" (22:1, 2).

SHIPHRAH: The king has said, "For as he thinketh in his heart, so is he: Eat and drink, saith he to thee; but his heart is not with thee" (23:7). He is my husband!

PERSIS: "If thou faint in the day of adversity, thy strength is small," Shiphrah (24:10).

NAAMAH: "Rejoice not when thine enemy falleth," Persis, "and let not thine heart be glad when he stumbleth: Lest the Lord see it, and it displease him, and he turn away" (24: 17, 18).

SHIPHRAH: If you call me your enemy, remember "these things also belong to the wise. It is not good to have respect of persons in judgment" (24:23).

PERSIS: "Take away the dross from the silver, and there shall come forth a vessel for the finer" (25:4).

NAAMAH: I do not seek a high place in my husband's court, "For better it is that it be said unto thee, Come up hither; than that thou shouldest be put lower in the presence of the prince whom thine eyes have seen" (25:7).

SHIPHRAH: I am weary with you two! How I miss my friends in Egypt! I long for news of home. "As cold waters to a thirsty soul, so is good news from a far country" (25:25).

NAAMAH: "Many seek the ruler's favour; but . . . judgment cometh from the Lord" (29:26). Neither your friends in Egypt nor your stone gods can help you now.

Devotional Object Talk

Think about families that you know, or your own family. Do you have a *perfect* family? Now think about families in the Bible. Were they perfect? Of course not! Families are made up of people, and people are not perfect.

The family unit is God's plan, though, to provide companionship for a man and a woman, and to nurture their children. The home is like a little splinter of heaven that God placed in the earth and wrapped families around it. It's the people in the home and their relationships to one another that make home a heaven or a hell on earth.

(*Write the letters F A M I L Y vertically on a chalkboard, or use six sheets of 8½ by 11 white paper with one of the letters from family printed on each page. As the talk proceeds, ·fill in the key words on the chalkboard; or hold up the individually lettered pages as you discuss each letter.*)

Think of the word *family*. F represents father, the head of the home, and M stands for mother, the heart of the home. Notice that A stands between father and mother and represents adjust. The blessings of home and marriage do not just happen, they are achieved by the adjustments that are made, the giving and receiving, the understanding and uplifting of each other.

I stands for image, or the impact of the home on members of the family, as well as neighbors and friends. What does your family stand for in your community? What influence do you have upon those around you? Do people see Jesus in your lives, do they feel the reflection of His light in your lives?

L stands for love, and family love involves much more than mere sex; it is consideration and kindness, long-suffering and patience, hard work and endurance. Family love is sweetness and sympathy, joy and joviality, faith and trust. Family love is based on God's love. It is God's way for His people to live together.

Y represents youth, the children that come to bless the home. What promise there is in the freshness of a newborn babe! What an awesome responsibility parents have as they help each little child to attain the high ideals of Christian maturity. Neither parent can do this alone—each must rely on God for strength and wisdom. If death or divorce has removed one parent, an extra burden is placed on the remaining members of the family.

Sometimes we are unaware of the good things in our lives. We are so busy with the daily details, we overlook the blessings of having a very special Book in our homes (*hold up the Bible*), and a watchful, loving Father in heaven who is concerned about the family.

Do not neglect these blessings in our world—the Book, the Author, the Family—available for all if we but seek and savor them. A *family* is the divine way for fulfilled human relationships.

Who Findeth a Husband

Parody of Proverbs 31

Who can find a loving husband, for his value far exceeds that of gardener, handyman, and financier?

The heart of his wife doth safely trust in him, whether in the presence of beguiling secretary or lonely woman seeking listening ear.

He spendeth more time at home than on golf course, bowling alley, or hunting trip.

He exerciseth restraint when bicycles and roller skates clutter driveway.

He accepteth strawberry-jelly kisses and peanut-butter hugs gladly.

He fixeth dump truck and disjointed Barbie doll with equal skill.

When wife screameth, he runneth to rescue and steppeth on black spider without ado.

He forgetteth not his wife's birthday and anniversary.

He noticeth his wife's new dress, hairdo, shoes, or purse and complimenteth her accordingly.

He showeth patience when new baby demandeth her time.

Shampoos, rinses, conditioners, assorted combs, curlers, and hair spray do leave him confused, but he pondereth them all in silence.

He is not the perfectionist that thinketh an occasional unmade bed or unwashed dish indicateth laziness.

He hangeth curtains and pictures, fixeth faucets, and repaireth steps promptly, then thanketh the Lord that his wife naggeth him not.

He goeth to Little League games and cheereth enthusiastically for son's team, whether winning or losing.

He patiently endureth piano, flute, clarinet, and violin lessons, and sitteth on front row at recital.

When in-laws come to visit he maketh them welcome.

He occasionally goeth shopping with wife and refraineth from grumbling, though lingerie and millinery appealeth to him not, and he secretly hopeth no other male seeth him.

When waiting for wife in car, he resisteth temptation to blow horn; upon departure, he accelerateth at normal speed.

He keepeth temper under control while helping children with modern math, and applaudeth grades received, but comprehendeth them not.

He refuseth not to attend P.T.A. meetings and Christmas programs.

He bestoweth affection lavishly on wife and children and remembereth to express appreciation verbally.

He exerciseth diplomacy and tact over length of hair and skirts.

He communicateth freely with wife, doth not pout and sulk during times of disagreement.

His strength supporteth family in times of crisis, yet he showeth tenderness and compassion.

He calmly accepteth wife's bewildering ways. Though he may never fully understand her, he loveth her just the same.

Meet him at the door with combed hair, powdered nose, and freshly pressed dress. Greet him with a smile, a kiss, and a warm welcome, for he is a priceless treasure.

—by Marilyn Habecker. *Eternity* Magazine. Used by permission.

Proverbial Hints for Happy Homes

Put God first

Trust in the Lord with all thine heart; and lean not unto thine own understanding. In all thy ways acknowledge him, and he shall direct thy paths.   —*Proverbs 3:5, 6*

Do your work willingly

She looketh well to the ways of her household, and eateth not the bread of idleness.   —*Proverbs 31:27*

Be slow to anger

He that is slow to anger is better than the mighty; and he that ruleth his spirit than he that taketh a city.   —*Proverbs 16:32*

Do not nag

It is better to dwell in the wilderness, than with a contentious and an angry woman.   —*Proverbs 21:19*

Do not speak too quickly

She openeth her mouth with wisdom; and in her tongue is the law of kindness.   —*Proverbs 31:26*

Do not be jealous

The heart of her husband doth safely trust in her.—*Proverbs 31:11*

Be cheerful and encouraging

A merry heart doeth good like a medicine: but a broken spirit drieth the bones.   —*Proverbs 17:22*

Be content

Better is a little with righteousness than great revenues without right.
                                                       —*Proverbs 16:8*

Nurture the children

The rod and reproof give wisdom: but a child left to himself bringeth his mother to shame. . . . Correct thy son, and he shall give thee rest; yea, he shall give delight unto thy soul.   —*Proverbs 29:15, 17*

Seek your husband's approval

A virtuous woman is a crown to her husband: but she that maketh ashamed is as rottenness in his bones.   —*Proverbs 12:4*

—From *Today's Christian Mother*. Used by permission.

CHAPTER VII

When Honesty Is Scorned

**"A false balance is abomination to the Lord:
but a just weight is his delight"
Proverbs 11:1**

THEME SONG: "True-Hearted, Whole-Hearted"

SCRIPTURE READING: Proverbs 11:1-11

PRAYER: Heavenly Father, we know Thou art good, for Thou
art God. And while we may not fully understand Thy
wondrous ways, we love and trust Thee, secure in the
knowledge that all things work together for good to them
that love Thee. Help us to be more honest in our daily
living, in the little ways, that we may uphold honor and
keep our integrity. Be with our leaders that they will not
be tempted to betray our trust in electing them to high
office. Guide them in their decisions so that our country
will continue to be great and honorable. In Jesus' name.
Amen.

Preparation: Cut out nine pieces of construction paper,
four inches square. Print one of the following occupations on
each square: homemaker, teacher, nurse, secretary, missionary,
lawyer, doctor, writer, editor. Paste on pictures of women

working at these jobs. Mention integrity problems for each one as you apply the squares with Plastic-Tak to a chart or chalkboard. Arrange them to form a twelve-inch square. You may wish to ask nine women in the group to comment briefly on each of the suggested occupations, if time allows.

The Square Christian

Square used to be a good word: you ate a square meal (satisfying); you stood foursquare (firm convictions); you were square with the world (owed no one); you could look a person square in the eye (honesty).

Then something happened to this wholesome word. Now it describes someone who volunteers when he doesn't have to; who tries harder and excels; someone who enjoys his work; one who is sentimental when the flag is unfurled; and one who is faithful to his God.

In January, 1964, Marya Mannes, writing in *McCalls*, said, "Today no one has to take any responsibility. The psychiatrists, the sociologists, the novelists, the playwrights have seen to that. Nobody really is to blame for what he does. It's Society. It's Environment. It's a Broken Home. It's an Underprivileged Area. But it's hardly ever You. . . . Right and wrong are a foreign language."

Almost a decade later, do you think the moral climate has improved?

While each one is "doing his own thing," obedience to God's laws are overlooked. A certain liberal minister allowed his congregation "to do their own thing": some people brought pets to church, one girl carrying a rabbit in its cage; many came barefoot and in bizarre clothing; they sang whatever songs they wished, indulged in whatever activity they wished, worshiped and believed whatever they wanted—the rule book was laid aside.

Do you think each one can do as he wishes and be in

the church established by the Son of God? Do you believe the rule book can be ignored? Yes, there is a guidebook for the Christian, and truly understanding and applying it to lives will produce the "square" Christian!

One of our early statesmen, Daniel Webster, was convinced that "all that is best in society today is the fruit of Christ's appearance among men. If we abide by the principles taught in the Bible, our country will go on prospering."

Let us define some terms. According to Webster, *integrity* implies trustworthiness and incorruptibility to a degree that one is incapable of being false to a trust, responsibility, or pledge. *Honor* suggests an active or anxious regard for the standards of one's profession or position. *Honesty* implies a refusal to lie, steal, or deceive in any way.

Problems of dishonesty are not new with our generation. The proverbs have much to say about integrity—it is an age-old problem of human nature!

"A false balance," a scales that cheat the customer, is "abomination to the Lord: but a just weight is his delight" (Proverbs 11:1). Do not be deceived, God knows about these things. He is interested in business deals, regarding with satisfaction the fair deals, with righteous indignation the tricks and fraudulent deals.

God knows when you hesitate or feel guilty, when white begins to look gray; whether you cheat or whether you are scrupulous in all your ways. "Life is a quarry, out of which we are to mold and chisel and complete a character" (Goethe).

God delights in this: "The integrity of the upright shall guide them" (Proverbs 11:3). Your honesty (or dishonesty) is recorded in the Lamb's book of life (Revelation 21:27), as well as in your own moral nature. You are stronger and better because of the willpower that comes with discipline in all matters of using "balanced scales" in your life.

The integrity of individuals reaches out to bless others: "By the blessing of the upright the city is exalted: but it is overthrown by the mouth of the wicked" (Proverbs 11:11). Or, consider this idea: "A man shall eat good by the fruit of his mouth: but the soul of the transgressors shall eat violence" (Proverbs 13:2).

Integrity also reaches out to members of the family: "The just man walketh in his integrity: his children are blessed after him" (Proverbs 20:7).

Oh, the importance of seemingly little things. Every look, every movement, every expression does something toward forming the character of a little child. "To make your children capable of honesty is the beginning of education" (Ruskin). Shakespeare wrote, "No legacy is so rich as honesty." Cicero, the Roman statesman, said, "What is becoming in behavior is honorable, and what is honorable is becoming." These are two of the refining qualities of civilization: honor and honesty.

Victor Hugo called progress the onward stride of God. When a nation loses its sense of history, and its dependence upon God, it is headed for destruction. Have you noticed that at school, history has become "social studies," and in many churches the good news has become a "social gospel." Most new books are concerned with current social problems. Doesn't this tend to imprison us in the present, with people failing to learn from history and ignoring eternal principles?

Arnold Toynbee, historian, says that of twenty-one civilizations, nineteen perished not from external conquest, but from the evaporation of belief within—belief in old-fashioned ideas like pride, patriotism, loyalty, hard work, faith in God.

"Good laws make it easier to do right and harder to do wrong."—Gladstone

"No people were ever better than their laws."—Priestley

Honesty Scorned

Several proverbs deal with the scorner, warning that "A scorner loveth not one that reproveth him: neither will he go unto the wise" (Proverbs 15:12). Sometimes it is wiser to let the scorner pass by—his bitter words can make wisdom appear ineffectual and helpless. The scorner can cover virtue with confusion that should belong only to vice.

The tragic heroine of the movie, *Days of Wine and Roses,* was ridiculed because she did not drink. She was made to feel ridiculous by her thoughtless young husband who could handle his drinking (so he thought). When she could no longer stand his scorn and that of their friends, she took her first drink, and to her husband's dismay and sorrow, became an alcoholic.

In characteristic pungent style, Proverbs 23:9 admonishes, "Speak not in the ears of a fool: for he will despise the wisdom of thy words." "The scorner is an abomination to men" (Proverbs 24:9).

Judy went to church camp one summer and came home committed to Christ. Her family made fun of her devotion and laughed at her Bible reading and prayers. She tried to share her fresh new faith with them, but was "turned off" coldly and cruelly. She loved her family and prayed that some day she could win them to Christ.

In the Sermon on the Mount, with vivid, uncomplimentary language, Jesus referred to this kind of rejection when He said, "Give not that which is holy unto the dogs, neither cast ye your pearls before swine, lest they trample them under their feet, and turn again and rend you" (Matthew 7:6). "Evil men understand not judgment: but they that seek the Lord understand all things" (Proverbs 28:5).

A thief's conscience does not bother him much, unless he is unsuccessful, or makes an error. Then his concern is that he should have been more careful, and that he will be caught! Stealing may start with taking a coin from Mother's purse: "Whoso robbeth his father or his mother, and saith, It is no transgression; the same is the companion of a destroyer" (Proverbs 28:24).

Conscience is not a safe guide unless it is informed and regulated by God's will and Word. A right intention is not enough to make a good action. We must measure our conduct by God's laws and not by what another person says or does. Neither praise nor scorn should determine our ways. We must learn to *act* instead of *react,* and not let other people shape our molds of conduct (Romans 12:2). God's judgment is not altered when we ignore it.

"Expedients are for the hour; principles for the ages" (Henry Ward Beecher). Abraham Lincoln said, "I am not bound to win, but I am bound to be true. I am not bound to succeed, but I must live up to the light I have."

"Honesty is the best policy" is not found in the Bible. This statement was made by Richard Whately (1787-1863) —and the rest of the quote is: ". . . but he who is governed by that maxim is not an honest man."

Honesty goes much deeper than being a policy. Dishonesty may also be the best policy, depending on your goal—if it is material prosperity, if it is cleverness in manipulation. God, however, does not judge by worldly standards and policies. His commands are succinctly stated: "Thou shalt not steal. Thou shalt not bear false witness" (Exodus 20:15, 16).

Remember the definitions earlier in this chapter? Notice how honor and humility are combined in Proverbs 15:33: "The fear of the Lord is the instruction of wisdom; and before honour is humility." The honorable person bows low before God, giving Him the honor and glory in all things, recognizing His majesty and greatness.

Discussion: Let's Be Honest

A college course in bookkeeping teaches all the tricks of "rigging" the books, so that fraud can be detected. Would not this also teach "how" to do it?

"A false balance is not good" (Proverbs 20:23).

Our women's council has a project of helping needy families. Must we always be giving to others? We have needs too!

"Whoso stoppeth his ears at the cry of the poor, he also shall cry himself, but shall not be heard" (Proverbs 21:13).

At the grocery store I mentioned an error to the checkout girl that cost me $1.00 extra. One of my friends laughed at me for doing this. Do you think honesty in little ways is important?

"Commit thy works unto the Lord, and thy thoughts shall be established" (Proverbs 16:3). "The scorner is an abomination" (Proverbs 24:9).

My car was involved in a minor accident that appeared to be my fault, but wasn't. When a bystander backed my version of the mishap, I did not receive a citation.

"A true witness delivereth souls: but a deceitful witness speaketh lies" (Proverbs 14:25).

It is difficult for the dishonest and the honest persons to get along, according to Proverbs 29:27: "An unjust man is an abomination to the just: and he that is upright in the way is abomination to the wicked." Discuss reasons for this.

Two quotes from *Othello*, by William Shakespeare:

> The Moor is of a free and open nature,
> That thinks men honest that but seem to be so.
> *Act I, scene 3, line 405*

> O wretched fool,
> That livest to make thine honesty a vice!
> O monstrous world! Take note, take note, O world,
> To be direct and honest is not safe.
> *Act III, scene 3, line 376*

Have someone review this great play and compare principles therein with Proverbs 17:4 and 21:6.

CHAPTER VIII

When Friends Fail You

"Faithful are the wounds of a friend;
but the kisses of an enemy are deceitful"
Proverbs 27:6

THEME SONG: "What a Friend We Have in Jesus"

SCRIPTURE READING: Proverbs 27:1-10

PRAYER: Our Father who is in heaven, how great Thou art! Thankful hearts rejoice in the coming of Thy Son, Jesus. What a friend He is in our daily lives! Guide us in our choice of earthly friends. Help us to be friendly and concerned about others and their needs. We thank Thee for Thy goodness. We praise Thy holy name. In Jesus' name we pray. Amen.

Preparation: Have two women prepare a debate on Proverbs 27:6: "Wounds of a Friend" versus "Kisses of an Enemy." Prepare poster slogans: "Kind Criticism—can you take it?" or "Fine Flattery—can you take it?" A lively discussion will be the result, especially if the two "debaters" have done their homework! Select two other ladies to present the following talks: "Value of a Friend" and "Friction With Friends."

Value of a Friend

Friends, according to the original meaning of the word, are those who delight in one another's company. They are compatible because each possesses gifts the other doesn't have, or they are agreeable because they have certain tastes in common; they are devoted to edifying one another.

Some friendships can be pledged to evil and destructive practices too, such as thieves entering into an arrangement to carry out their plans, or neighbors conspiring as a clique to shut out other neighbors. They may be very true to each other. Even vicious people can find a common bond of friendship in their vices—"friends for mutual shattering" as someone has said.

Do you believe that friendship cemented together with sin can long endure? Can trust ever be a part of such a relationship? Discuss.

When we think of friendship, however, we usually mean that bond of loyalty and love that tends to bless, strengthen, and improve people. It is the response of kindred hearts, recognizing mutual ideas, and

> As in water face answereth to face,
> so the heart of man to man.
> —*Proverbs 27:19*

Isn't that a beautiful analogy! When you look into a clear pool of water and see the reflection of your face, it is like looking into the heart of a friend and seeing there something of yourself.

> When friendships, love and truth abound,
>   Among a band of brothers,
> The cup of joy goes daily around,
>   Each shares the bliss of others.
> How grand in age, how fair in youth
>   Are holy friendships, love and truth!
> —*Author Unknown*

Friends—Christian friends—will reach out to become help-fully interested in other people. Loving the same Lord brings people close together.

Dale Carnegie wrote, "You can make more friends in two months by becoming interested in other people than you can in two years by trying to get other people interested in you."

Few develop the kind of earthly relationship that brings "the inexpressible comfort of feeling safe with a person; having neither to weigh thoughts nor measure words, but to pour them all out, just as they are, chaff and grain together, knowing that a faithful hand will take and sift them, keep what is worth keeping, and then, with the breath of kindness, blow the rest away" (George Eliot).

This is the blessed kind of friendship, approaching the divine ideal found only in Christ.

When a friendship develops through the years, most of the pain of mutual correction is gone and

> Ointment and perfume rejoice the heart:
> so doth the sweetness of a . . . friend.
> —*Proverbs 27:9*

There is a gentleness and consideration for the feelings of each other that becomes sweeter as the years pass. Often you do not know your real friends until a need arises. When calamity comes, false friends make excuses and leave you; lip-friends lapse into silence; but true friends will appear to aid and comfort.

> A friend loveth at all times, and a brother
> is born for adversity.
> —*Proverbs 17:17*

Their help may take the place of a brother who lives far away.

> Thine own friend, and thy father's friend,
> forsake not; . . . for better is a neighbour
> that is near than a brother far off.
> —*Proverbs 27:10*

If you have real friends like this, be sure to keep them close—let no difference come between you. Such friendship in the earthly relationship is used by Jesus to explain the loftier relationship of Christian love. Jesus Christ is our nearest and dearest friend.

> A man that hath friends must shew himself friendly: and there is a friend that sticketh closer than a brother.
> —*Proverbs 18:24*

Friction With Friends

> Iron sharpeneth iron; so a man sharpeneth the countenance of his friend.
> —*Proverbs 27:17*

The simile of iron reminds us that there is a discipline in friendship that may be accompanied by pain. Friends "rub down each other's angles," and the friction may hurt some!

The iron becomes dull of edge when kept from the sharpening process, so friends separated grow dull. As iron becomes sharp and bright by friction, so the meeting of friends tends to sharpen and polish the understanding and lighten the heart.

A woman without friends has a lonely look, and her conversation has a dull edge. Reading books may make her learned, but not social or friendly. Friendships do not flower overnight. They require cultivation and time.

George Washington said, "True friendship is a plant of slow growth, and must undergo and withstand the shocks of adversity before it is entitled to the appellation." Deep personal ties are formed during times of trouble. People are led to know each other better, and to know God better too.

Fellowship is a form of friendship. You help shape society by your behavior, and are shaped yourself by social contacts. As a parent you find yourself reflected in your children. As a teacher you give something of yourself to your students.

As a friend you share something of your personality with friends. These relationships can lead to friction as well as harmony.

Proverbs 16:28, 29 and 17:9 warn about a special habit that leads to friction with friends. "He that repeats a matter separates friends." (Chapter IV discusses "When Your Tongue Is Careless.")

A type of "boisterous friendship" is described by this proverb: "He that blesseth his friend with a loud voice, rising early in the morning, it shall be counted a curse to him" (Proverbs 27:14). How would you respond to a friend whose telephone call—even with a compliment—blasted you out of bed early in the morning? This could place a strain upon the bonds of affection you have for each other!

Then there's the false friend who likes to flatter you, and against whom the proverb warns: "A man that flattereth his neighbour spreadeth a net for his feet" (Proverbs 29:5).

The gossipy friend: "He that goeth about as a talebearer revealeth secrets" (Proverbs 20:19), and the violent person:

> Make no friendship with an angry man;
> and with a furious man thou shalt not go:
> Lest thou learn his ways,
> and get a snare to thy soul.
> —*Proverbs 22:24, 25*

Some people can cause so much friction in your life, it may be well to take the advice given the young fox in an ancient fable. The little fox asked his father to teach him some tricks to help defeat the dogs if he should be chased by them. Even though Father Fox's fur was gray from a long life of danger, and his scars showed marks of narrow escapes from the dog packs, he replied with a sigh, "After all my experience, I am forced to confess that often the best trick is to keep out of their way!"

One of the proverbs, with sharp humor, says, "Withdraw thy foot from thy neighbour's house; lest he be weary of thee, and so hate thee" (Proverbs 25:17). "Visit seldom and they love thee more," or "Familiarity breeds contempt," are ancient adages that deserve contemplation.

Another way to cause friction between friends is through business or money matters. A summary of Proverbs 6:1-5 would be "do not borrow or lend to a friend"——he who pays another man's debts seeketh his own decay. To be "surety" for a friend is very likely to bring problems and a wedge between friends so that "Thou art snared with words." This refers to verbal agreements, but even a signed contract or note can make a dear friend into an enemy. (*Also read Proverbs 11:15.*)

When earthly friends fail you, remember that Jesus is a friend. Choosing friends that also claim Him as Lord, Saviour, and friend will lead you to have solid and true Christian friends on this earth too.

Quotes for Discussion

1. He who has one thousand friends
     has not a friend to spare,
   And he who has one enemy
     will meet him everywhere.——Emerson
2. Wrath is cruel, and anger is outrageous;
     but who is able to stand before envy?——Proverbs 27:4
   How does envy affect friendship?
3. Do you believe that nine out of every ten people improve on acquaintance? Discuss.
4. Do you agree: It's funny, but true,
                  Folks you don't like,
                  Don't like you.
5. "We boil at different degrees." How does this tendency affect friendship?

CHAPTER IX

When Wine Sparkles

**"Wine is a mocker, strong drink is raging:
and whosoever is deceived thereby is not wise"
Proverbs 20:1**

THEME SONG: "Yield Not to Temptation"

SCRIPTURE READING: Proverbs 23:29-35

PRAYER: Father in heaven, we thank Thee for flowers and food, for sunshine and rain. We thank Thee for the harvest and golden grain. Forgive those who misuse these blessings to produce something that harms mankind. We pray for the homes where the problem of alcoholism destroys peace of mind and happiness. We ask that people in high places will do something about a national problem of drinking. Help each of us to do what we can where we are to alleviate the pain of problem drinkers. In Jesus' name. Amen.

Special Feature: Invite a policeman or a social worker to be your guest, relating experiences in dealing with the problem drinker. Or, have a report on up-to-date statistics for the cost of alcoholism to your city and/or state.

Prepare a poster of the positive uses of the fruit of the vine:

grape juice, jelly, gourmet recipes, the emblems of the Lord's Supper. An artistic member could prepare humorous "self-control" cartoons that correlate with the theme.

Fruit of the Vine

Do you have childhood memories of a grape arbor where you spent summer hours in verdant shade? Do you recall how, as the fruit ripened, you could reach up, pick a cluster of grapes and enjoy a succulent treat from God's creative hand? Or, possibly you have made grape jelly, or canned the juice, delicious on winter evenings served with pop corn. Tantalizing products can be made from the fruit of the vine!

What a beautiful sight a vineyard is! The modern traveler in Israel visits vineyards that stretch in well kept rows as far as the eye can see. The fruit is a reminder of the experiences of the spies sent by Moses who arrived in Canaan at the "time of the firstripe grapes." What bountiful evidence they found of a fruitful land! "They came unto the brook of Eshcol, and cut down from thence a branch with one cluster of grapes, and they bare it between two upon a staff" (Numbers 13:23).

How did God want mankind to use these beautiful grapes? In a land where water was scarce and fruit juice could be plentiful, what do you suppose mankind learned to drink? (*Think about this—then discuss.*)

Throughout the Bible there seems to be an important emphasis on the fruit of the vine, literally and symbolically. (*You may wish to prepare a special study of the Lord's Supper and the emblems used.*) This luscious fruit, among many others, was provided for mankind to enjoy. The colorful juice was delightful to look upon, and delectable to the taste, but it also "biteth like a serpent, and stingeth like an adder" (Proverbs 23:32).

As with other blessings of God, this one too can become a curse to mankind. The Old Testament records several drunken scenes involving venerable patriarchs: Noah, Genesis 9:20, 21; David and Uriah, 2 Samuel 11:13.

Isn't it strange that indulgence in many of the "sparkling" things of life interfere with spiritual growth? The glittering neon signs that entice the passerby lead into dark depths of dancing and drinking. Glistening waters of the lake or river lure good people away from the church on Sunday, to catch that shiny fish, to lift that sparkling glass.

"Who hath woe? who hath sorrow? who hath contentions? who hath babbling? who hath wounds without cause? who hath redness of eyes?" (Proverbs 23:29). Not all who drink wine fall into the condition described here. The answer to the six questions is given in one sentence: "They that tarry long at the wine; they that go to seek mixed wine" (Proverbs 23:30). Lingering over the drink, spending hours, mixing and sampling, not the use so much as the abuse causes the woe.

Who is to know where that limit is between use and abuse? There is no built-in monitor that reminds the drinker. When a beverage seems most pleasant to see and to taste, the proverb warns: "Look not thou upon the wine when it is red, when it giveth his colour in the cup, when it moveth itself aright" (Proverbs 23:31). The tingle of a pleasant indulgence that seemed to be perfectly innocent can be a deceiver: "Wine is a mocker, strong drink is raging: and whosoever is deceived thereby is not wise" (Proverbs 20:1).

Excessive drinking leads to the destruction of every faculty that God has provided to protect man from danger and guide him through life. Perception is marred, the will paralyzed, and conscience dies. "Thou shalt be as he that lieth down in the midst of the sea, or as he that lieth upon the top of a mast" (Proverbs 23:34). The intoxicant does not remember what happened: "They have stricken me, shalt thou say, and I was not sick, they have beaten me, and I felt it not" (Proverbs 23:35). And the most pathetic result is, "When shall I awake? I will seek it yet again" (Proverbs 23:35).

The desire for pleasures that "sparkle" can be mastered only by turning to the Master. True temperance is one of the fruits of the Spirit, and is of little value unless accompanied by love, joy, peace, long-suffering, gentleness, goodness, faith, meekness (Galatians 5:22, 23). True temperance involves self-control.

(If the "self-control" cartoons have been prepared as suggested on page 70, mention them at this time and discuss their application to life. The problem of adequate self-control affects many areas of daily living.)

Fooled by Wine

Naturally fermented wines probably antedate agriculture. The process required no special ingenuity of man—nature quickly made wine from berries left in some primitive piece of pottery. Wine may be any fruit juice, usually of the grape, that has been fermented through exposure to yeast germs in the air, producing ethyl alcohol. Carbonic acid gas is shown in the bubbles that appear, or as described in Proverbs 23:31, "moveth itself."

Anything that nature has supplied with sugar has been brewed by mankind (this has taken a peculiar ingenuity!): fruits, berries, saps of cactus and palm, milk of mare and goat, grain, including rice and corn.

Wine fools people because the alcohol in it does not show the same effect on all who drink it. They do not know or understand the chemical action. Because of its narcotic nature, alcohol begins its destruction by dimming, then dulling, finally deadening the nervous system.

Since alcohol does not need to be digested, it is absorbed almost immediately into the blood, and thus to the brain. Its first effect is to dull intelligence, then relax self-control. This characteristic contributes to its effectiveness as an ingredient in prescriptions. The medicine circulates quickly.

Listen to these figures:
 2-6% of beer is alcohol
 6-8% of ale is alcohol
 12-23% of wine is alcohol
 40-50% of distilled spirits is alcohol
 60-65% of some liqueurs (absinthe) is alcohol
Alcohol is a depressant. Consumed in sufficient quantity it will put the person to sleep.

Wine makes fools of people by these stages of intoxication:
 1. *Euphoria,* a feeling of well-being. The cares of the world do not bother, and moral codes do not bind, so people do things they would not ordinarily do.
 2. *Incoordination,* becoming talkative, boastful. The body begins to sway because brain centers controlling the legs are affected.
 3. *Confusion,* leading to staggering. The tongue thickens, movements are slow and deliberate—the person is drunk.
 4. *Anesthesia,* stuporous, asleep, unconscious. The inebriate can only be aroused with difficulty; he cannot stand on his feet without help.
 5. *Death.* Man is created so that he becomes unconscious or asleep as described in number four. But if the blood alcohol reaches 0.5% or over, death knocks at the door.

Why do people drink? Custom or culture provides four reasons for drinking:
 1. Ritual drinking—religious ceremony
 2. Dietary drinking—mealtime
 3. Convivial drinking—pleasure, social
 4. Utilitarian—business transactions, sealing a deal
The individual may drink for one or more of these reasons also: to bolster his self-esteem; to remove tension; to dispel threat of danger; to achieve pleasure or social status; to cover feelings of guilt.

"Alcohol is the liquid that loosens up our leisure life and louses up our spiritual life."

Some advertising fools people into thinking drinking is the "in" thing to do. Wine is associated with wealth, prestige, and power. The sordid side, the sickness, the sorrow resulting from the drinking problem receive little publicity. Man's attitude toward alcohol has always been ambivalent, neither wholly approving nor wholly abstaining.

One interesting group of people in the Old Testament that practiced total abstinence, according to family tradition, was the Rechabites, in-laws of Moses (Jeremiah 35:6-10). Another select group who took vows to abstain were the Nazarites, meaning "separation unto the Lord." Outstanding Biblical characters who took the Nazarite vow (Numbers 6: 1-21) were: Samson (Judges 13:2-7); Samuel (1 Samuel 1:11); and John the Baptist (Luke 1:15). Sometimes this arrangement was made with God before the birth of the child, and women could also take the vow.

Here is a proverb that seems designed for the one who must be understanding with the alcoholic: "If thou faint in the day of adversity, thy strength is small" (Proverbs 24:10). And this one seems designed for the Christian who should be an example: "A righteous man falling down before the wicked is as a troubled fountain, and a corrupt spring" (Proverbs 25:26). And this one includes many areas of self-control: "He that hath no rule over his own spirit is like a city that is broken down, and without walls" (Proverbs 25:28).

In Proverbs 31:4-7 we learn that it is foolish for kings or princes to drink wine, "Lest they drink, and forget the law, and pervert the judgment." Verses six and seven seem to indicate two instances when the use of wine was encouraged: medicinal and for mourners. It was a Jewish custom to give a cup of wine to the bereaved.

Finally, if wine doesn't tempt you, don't be smug! Mentally substitute the word that does fit. Maybe your weakness

is potato chips, peanuts, homemade fudge—any overindul-
gence can be detrimental to health. Notice that Jesus placed
overeating, overdrinking, and worry in the same category
(Luke 21:34).

Fooled by wine? Fooled by some other indulgence? Convinced "it" won't happen to you? Practice self-control!

Discussion

1. How is the use of alcohol affecting family life in the
   United States? Find current statistics.
2. Discuss "The wise through excess is made a fool" (Emer-
   son). Proverbs 3:21-26 suggests the way to maintain self-
   control in all temptations.
3. Do you believe intemperate use of alcohol is deceitful?
   Consider Proverbs 20:1. Discuss these two ways that ad-
   vertisers use to extol advantages: (a) improves sociability;
   (b) enriches national revenue.
4. Read Proverbs 4:17-19. Discuss the metaphors, the contrast of the way of the wicked and the path of the just.
   Notice specific sins are not mentioned.
5. Read these four lines and apply the thought to the theme
   of this chapter:
   > There is a line by us unseen
   >   That crosses every path,
   > The hidden boundary between
   >   God's patience and His wrath.

CHAPTER X

When Leadership Falters

**"When thou sittest to eat with a ruler,
consider diligently what is before thee"
Proverbs 23:1**

THEME SONG: "Where He Leads Me"

SCRIPTURE READING: Proverbs 8:23-36

PRAYER: Father in heaven, help us to be good followers, able to discern the quality of the leadership. Guide the people elected to places of leadership in our country, state, city, women's group. Be with the minister, elders, deacons, Bible-school teachers, and officers that their leadership will extol Thy name and teach Thy ways. In Jesus' name we pray. Amen.

Preparation: Make this a patriotic meeting, using red, white, and blue decorations, and displaying both the Christian flag and the national flag. Prepare a report on countries that still have a king. Discuss their international image. If you make copies of the "Leadership Litany" so that all can participate, include the name of this book and author, to protect the copyright.

The Glory of a King

What picture comes to your mind when you hear the word "king"? Do you see him as a figure of power and wealth? Do you think of a gold palace and a jeweled crown? Do you think of King Solomon, his wealth, wives, and wisdom?

In the time that the Proverbs were written and compiled, most nations had kings, and some of them were looked upon as gods. "A divine sentence is in the lips of the king: his mouth transgresseth not in judgment" (Proverbs 16:10). Loyal subjects thought the throne was divinely established (Proverbs 16:12-15).

Egypt was one of the ancient countries that considered the king a god. The custom made its way into other Mediterranean areas. One time when King Herod, arrayed in royal apparel, made an oration in Caesarea, "the people gave a shout, saying, It is the voice of a god, and not of a man" (Acts 12:22). Read verse twenty-three also to see what the angel of the Lord did to Herod!

> The glories of our blood and state
> Are shadows, not substantial things;
> There is no armour against fate;
> Death lays his icy hand on kings:
> > Sceptre and crown
> > Must tumble down,
> And in the dust be equal made
> With the poor crooked scythe and spade.
> —James Shirley, 1596-1666

When Israel asked for a king "that we also may be like all the nations," Samuel warned the people (1 Samuel 8: 6-22). "You will be oppressed," he said. "You will not be happy with a king."

God allowed a king to be chosen. From that time the king of Israel was a type and a foreshadow of the anointed King, the Christ, who would come to earth one day.

In both the historical and wisdom books, the ideal elements of the kings referred to the coming King of kings; the actual shortcomings of the kings, the evil they did, was a cruel contrast to the Christ who would reign over hearts. However, even bad rulers played their part in God's plan.

The wisdom book of Proverbs has much to say about the glory and honor of a king. He represented righteousness: "the throne is established by righteousness" (Proverbs 16:12). He sat on a throne of judgment: "A king that sitteth in the throne of judgment scattereth away all evil with his eyes" (Proverbs 20:8); "A wise king scattereth the wicked, and bringeth the wheel over them" (Proverbs 20:26). The ideal king encouraged the righteous: "He that loveth pureness of heart, for the grace of his lips the king shall be his friend" (Proverbs 22:11).

The anger of a king is as "messengers of death: but a wise man will pacify it" (Proverbs 16:14). What a marvelous metaphor is in Proverbs 19:12: "The king's wrath is as the roaring of a lion; but his favour is as dew upon the grass." A human king will make mistakes, with sin and suffering as the result. The heavenly King can sift the faithful from the faithless. He has all authority in heaven and earth.

Other kingly proverbs for consideration:

Proverbs 14:35	Proverbs 23:1-5
Proverbs 16:14, 15	Proverbs 24:21, 22
Proverbs 19:6-12	Proverbs 25:2-7
Proverbs 20:2, 5-8, 26, 28	Proverbs 29:14
Proverbs 21:1-4	Proverbs 30:24-31

No earthly king ever fulfilled this ideal concept of a monarch. There is only one way of explaining the language of these eloquent proverbs—they point to Christ. There is a sublime mixture of imagery, some quite earthly, others uniquely heavenly. Most of them require study and wisdom to comprehend.

Listen to chapter 29 of Proverbs: "When the righteous are in authority, the people rejoice: but when the wicked beareth rule, the people mourn (2) . . . The king by judgment establisheth the land: but he that receiveth gifts overthroweth it (4) . . . If a ruler hearken to lies, all his servants are wicked (12) . . . The king that faithfully judgeth the poor, his throne shall be established for ever (14). . . . Where there is no vision, the people perish: but he that keepeth the law, happy is he (18). . . . Many seek the ruler's favour; but every man's judgment cometh from the Lord (26)."

The trends of good and evil kings are reflected in the Proverbs. Some of the evils, or errors, are in these verses:

Proverbs 14:28   Proverbs 29:2, 4
Proverbs 15:22   Proverbs 30:22
Proverbs 17:7   Proverbs 31:4-9
Proverbs 28:2, 12, 15, 16

Fleshly vices tempted and led many rulers astray, away from their regal responsibilities.

Every human heart seeks loyalty to a suitable figure of authority. If it does not find the King of kings, it will turn to a "pretender." Jesus came in humility. His appeal is to the heart, not the eye. False kings dazzle the eye and blind us to the majesty of the Sovereign who reigns above.

A Leadership Litany

The following oral, responsive reading, will provide humor and program variety, as proverbs are applied to modern-day problems.

LEADER: Sometimes I am weary with committee meetings. Why do we have to discuss so much?

RESPONSE: Where no counsel is, the people fall: but in the multitude of counsellors there is safety. . . . Without counsel purposes are disappointed: but in the multitude of counsellors they are established (Proverbs 11:14; 15:22).

ALL: The path of the just is as the shining light, that shineth more and more unto the perfect day (Proverbs 4:18).

LEADER: When I hear some news about one of our members, should I repeat it?

RESPONSE: A talebearer revealeth secrets: but he that is of a faithful spirit concealeth the matter (Proverbs 11: 13).

ALL: Bread of deceit is sweet to a man; but afterwards his mouth shall be filled with gravel (Proverbs 20:17).

LEADER: Sometimes I am tired of "following," but I really don't want to lead either!

RESPONSE: It is not good to eat much honey: so for men to search their own glory is not glory (Proverbs 25:27).

ALL: The fear of the Lord is the instruction of wisdom; and before honour is humility (Proverbs 15:33).

LEADER: We don't have much money in the treasury . . . How can we increase the giving in our group? Why do we have so many money problems?

RESPONSE: Better is a little with righteousness than great revenues without right. . . . How much better is it to get wisdom than gold! and to get understanding rather to be chosen than silver! (Proverbs 16:8, 16).

ALL: Better is little with the fear of the Lord than great treasure and trouble therewith (Proverbs 15:16).

LEADER: What a problem for the executive committee! I hope they find the answer.

RESPONSE: He that handleth a matter wisely shall find good: and whoso trusteth in the Lord, happy is he (Proverbs 16:20).

ALL: Understanding is a wellspring of life unto him that hath it: but the instruction of fools is folly (Proverbs 16:22).

Leader: Our president handled that business meeting capably. What was her secret of success?

Response: Pleasant words are as an honeycomb, sweet to the soul, and health to the bones (Proverbs 16:24).

All: The thoughts of the wicked are an abomination to the Lord: but the words of the pure are pleasant words (Proverbs 15:26).

Leader: Yes, her pleasant words turned off anger and disagreement among our members.

Response: He that is slow to anger is better than the mighty; and he that ruleth his spirit than he that taketh a city (Proverbs 16:32).

All: The beginning of strife is as when one letteth out water: therefore leave off contention, before it be meddled with (Proverbs 17:14).

Leader: Followers will never go farther than their leaders. Good leaders are essential to spiritual growth.

Response: The simple believeth every word: but the prudent man looketh well to his going (Proverbs 14:15).

All: Ponder the path of thy feet, and let all thy ways be established (Proverbs 4:26).

Leader: What a joy it is to call on some of our shut-ins! They help me more than I help them!

Response: A merry heart maketh a cheerful countenance: but by sorrow of the heart the spirit is broken. . . . All the days of the afflicted are evil: but he that is of a merry heart hath a continual feast (Proverbs 15:13, 15).

All: The spirit of a man will sustain his infirmity; but a wounded spirit who can bear? (Proverbs 18:14).

Leader: One of my friends wants to follow Jesus; she needs someone to encourage her. I want to help, but . . .

RESPONSE: A man hath joy by the answer of his mouth: and
a word spoken in due season, how good is it! . . . A man's
heart deviseth his way: but the Lord directeth his steps
(Proverbs 15:23; 16:9).

ALL: Death and life are in the power of the tongue: and
they that love it shall eat the fruit thereof (Proverbs 18:
21).

Discussion

1. Jesus said, "Render to Caesar the things that are Caesar's,
and to God the things that are God's" (Mark 12:17). In
Hebrews 13:17 we read, "Obey them that have the rule
over you." Apply these concepts to good citizenship and
the proverbs studied in this chapter.
2. A good leader sees: (a) what ought to be done; (b) what
can be done; (c) how to do it. "Seest thou a man diligent
in his business? he shall stand before kings" (Proverbs
22:29). Also consider Proverbs 27:23-27.
3. Can a weak leader be as ineffective as a wicked leader?
4. Liberty is the right to do what the laws allow; and if a
citizen could do what they forbid, it would be no longer
liberty, because others would have the same powers.

—Montesquieu

5. Discuss: A good thing to remember
And a better thing to do:
To work with the construction gang
And not with the wrecking crew.

Apply this thought to leaders and followers.

CHAPTER XI

When Your Neighbor Needs Help

"He that passeth by, and meddleth with strife belonging not to him, is like one that taketh a dog by the ears"
Proverbs 26:17

THEME SONG: "Make Me a Blessing"

SCRIPTURE READING: Proverbs 26:17-28

PRAYER: Dear heavenly Father, make me a blessing to my neighbor. Help me to allow my neighbor to be a blessing to me. Guide me in the words, the actions, the gifts I offer and make my motives to be honest and helpful. We thank Thee for Jesus who taught us who our neighbors really are. We need guidance in so many things of this life! We praise Thy holy name, praying in the name of Jesus. Amen.

Preparation: For the Bible-times devotional, read responsively the neighborly "Notes From Wives" with the responses from Proverbs. These could be typed on stationery as letters (or scrolls) to King Solomon, with the proverbs used in reply. This could also be used as a dialogue.

For the modern-day application to neighborliness, use the dialogue, " 'Tis More Blessed to Give Than to Receive." This brief, humorous skit should stimulate a discussion of the reasons for calling, the importance of motivation and method in relationships with others.

Notes From Wives

QUESTION SCROLL FOR KING SOLOMON: Mrs. Tell-it-all lives next door to me. Sometimes I feel bruised by the gossip she tells me, and the awareness that she will tell others about my business. Why did you add such a woman to your harem? O my king, I realize it was to receive the goodwill of her father's kingdom, but what words of wisdom do you have for me?

PROVERBS FOR THE DAY: As a mad man who casteth fire-brands, arrows, and death, so is the man that deceiveth his neighbour, and saith, Am not I in sport? Where no wood is, there the fire goeth out: so where there is no talebearer, the strife ceaseth (Proverbs 26:18-20). An hypocrite with his mouth destroyeth his neighbour: but through knowledge shall the just be delivered (Proverbs 11:9).

QUESTION SCROLL FOR KING SOLOMON: Mrs. Borrow-a-candle bothers me every day with a request for something. Her gods are strange and her ways of worship annoy me. I love my God. I would like to help her add this important ingredient to her life—faith in the living God—so I try to be patient and long-suffering with her borrowing.

PROVERBS FOR THE DAY: Say not unto thy neighbour, Go, and come again, and to morrow I will give; when thou hast it by thee (Proverbs 3:28). A gift is as a precious stone in the eyes of him that hath it: whithersoever it turneth, it prospereth (Proverbs 17:8).

QUESTION SCROLL FOR KING SOLOMON: Mrs. Stay-a-while comes to see me on my busiest day. I try to be nice to her but she really bothers me. She tries to fix all my frustrations with her platitudes and advice. Her Persian gods bore me. Meanwhile my day is gone and my peace of mind is disturbed.

PROVERBS FOR THE DAY: He that passeth by, and meddleth with strife belonging not to him, is like one that taketh a dog by the ears (Proverbs 26:17). When a man's ways please the Lord, he maketh even his enemies to be at peace with him (Proverbs 16:7).

QUESTION SCROLL FOR KING SOLOMON: Mrs. False Witness not only tells it all, she does not tell the truth, O king. She causes friction and quarrels and none of us like her. Some of your wives would like to get even with her. This is causing a difficult problem in our household. What do you suggest?

PROVERBS FOR THE DAY: A man that beareth false witness against his neighbor is a maul, and a sword, and a sharp arrow (Proverbs 25:18). Be not a witness against thy neighbour without cause; and deceive not with thy lips. Say not, I will do so to him as he hath done to me: I will render to the man according to his work (Proverbs 24:28, 29). Devise not evil against thy neighbour, seeing he dwelleth securely by thee (Proverbs 3:29).

QUESTION SCROLL FOR KING SOLOMON: Mrs. Calamity Kate delights in telling me all the bad things that happen in the harem. I am teaching my children to look for the good things in their daily lives. We play a game every evening called "something good happened today." O king, what do you have to say about this problem?

PROVERBS FOR THE DAY: Whoso mocketh the poor reproach-
eth his Maker: and he that is glad at calamities shall not
be unpunished (Proverbs 17:5). He that is void of wisdom despiseth his neighbour: but a man of understanding
holdeth his peace (Proverbs 11:12).

SUMMARY SCROLL: Mrs. Nearby Neighbor is a dear little
lady whom I seldom see, yet we enjoy each other's company very much. We share hobbies, we talk about our love
of God. One day I said, "I'm a terrible neighbor! I'm
too busy to visit much." Her reply was precious: "That's
the best kind of neighbor." Do you agree? (Discuss.)

RESPONSE: It is the quality of neighborliness, not the quantity
that is important. To know a neighbor is there, to visit
and to share—without excess—this is rich companionship
in a local community.

> To love the whole world for me is no chore;
> My biggest problem is the neighbor next door!

Prayer: Give us the gift of being a good neighbor. Let
our love of God be seen by all who know us and would
seek to follow Thee.   Amen.

A Modern-day Dialogue

This dialogue can be presented without rehearsal. Have
copies prepared with RECEIVER underlined in red; GIVER
underlined in blue, for easy reading of the roles. Place a pie
plate inside a brown paper sack. GIVER holds this package
until the last speech is made.

Some ladies may want to practice the skit, even to learn
the speeches. Of course, this will add to the dramatic possi-
bilities. The main idea, however, is to present in an exagger-
ated way, some new thoughts on a familiar situation: giving
and receiving.

'TIS MORE BLESSED TO GIVE THAN TO RECEIVE

GIVER (*holding something in a brown paper sack*): I brought something for you.

RECEIVER: What is it?

GIVER: Oh, it's just a pie.

RECEIVER: It is? Why did you bring me a pie?

GIVER: Well, I thought you'd like to have a pie, so I brought you one.

RECEIVER: I guess I should just take it and say thank you. But why be cut and dried? Let's talk about this pie.

GIVER: You don't like my pies?

RECEIVER: Frankly, I've had better. But that's not the point. Even if your pie were an exceptionally good pie, I still wonder why you want to give me a pie.

GIVER: I felt I ought to help you over this rough spot. You have your troubles now. And besides you help people too, when you can.

RECEIVER: This is a way of paying me back?

GIVER: That's putting it rather bluntly.

RECEIVER: Well, shall we say you feel indebted to me, and you would rather have me indebted to you.

GIVER: Are you inferring that I'm trying to better myself by giving you this pie?

RECEIVER: Yes, that's one way of saying it. I really think your need to give is bigger than my need to receive.

GIVER: It is?

RECEIVER: Yes. Even though my children are sick; the water company cut off our water; we got our last unemployment check last month; and we haven't had bread for two days —the answer is still yes.

GIVER: For a hungry person, you're sure philosophical.

RECEIVER: To be hungry makes one philosophical, or bitter!

GIVER: Do you think it is wrong for me to be giving you this pie?

RECEIVER: Certainly not, and especially if it's rhubarb. But, really now, why did you think of bringing me a pie?

GIVER: Well, I noticed that we had two pies and remembered that you probably had none. It just didn't seem right.

RECEIVER: You felt guilty about having so many pies? If you give me one, you won't feel so guilty about still having one pie, plus one cake, three boxes of assorted crackers and cookies, a gallon of ice cream, and a refrigerator full of leftovers?

GIVER: You're drooling on the sack.

RECEIVER: You're avoiding the question.

GIVER: You're not my psychiatrist, either.

RECEIVER: Sorry.

GIVER: Don't you believe it's more blessed to give than to receive? That's what it says in the Bible: Acts 20:35.

RECEIVER: Perhaps so, but we receivers needs a lot of grace. It's not easy to take all this stuff and keep our self-respect. But it helps me to remember that I'm giving you givers something by taking what you offer.

GIVER: That's real considerate of you. You'll take the pie?

RECEIVER: Did you ever doubt it? Now let's get to the point.

GIVER (*still holding the pie*): The pie is getting heavy.

RECEIVER: I suspect that you want me to come to your church.

GIVER: Well, yes.

RECEIVER: I don't know whether I like being bribed with a crummy old pie.

GIVER: It's cherry.

RECEIVER: That's the best kind of a bribe, except for rhubarb.

GIVER: Sure, I want you to come to our church. But whether you ever do or not, I want to give you this pie.

RECEIVER: I like you. You're kind of honest.

GIVER: You've driven me to it.

RECEIVER: You've made me feel like somebody, not just a pie-taker.

GIVER (*holding out the sack*): I'd like to ask you to do something for me.

RECEIVER (*taking the brown paper sack*): Yes?

GIVER: The next time I give you something, please just say thank you and shut up!

—From *The Mennonite*. Used by permission.

Discussion

1. If you are always the giver, have you ever considered how the receiver feels? Do you find it difficult to receive gifts gracefully?

2. Proverbs 25:8 seems to summarize the dialogue situation. Should the giver stop giving? Should the helper stop helping? Can we help people too much?

3. Read Luke 10:25-42 to see what Jesus said about neighbors.

4. How can I let my light shine so that others will be attracted, not blinded or overwhelmed by my piety?

5. Discuss the following statements:

> If you want to be rich, give.
> If you want to be poor, grasp.
> If you want abundance, scatter.
> If you want to be needy, hoard.

CHAPTER XII

When Virtue Is Vanishing

**"Discretion shall preserve thee,
understanding shall keep thee"
Proverbs 2:11**

THEME SONG: "Purer in Heart"

SCRIPTURE READING: Proverbs 5:1-14; Philippians 4:7, 8

PRAYER: O God, how glorious are Thy works, how wonderful Thy name! When we see that many people seek to destroy the beauty of the world and their own bodies through sin, we are sickened. We ask forgiveness. Help us to persevere in a self-seeking society. Help us to use our bodies as Thou intended. Make in us a temple where Thou canst dwell. In Jesus' name. Amen.

Preparation: Make this a "heart" meeting, emphasizing the importance of the pure heart (Matthew 5:8) and lofty thoughts (Philippians 4:7, 8). For presenting the "Heart Beauty Shop," prepare large hearts from red construction paper, or draw with red felt pen, a heart-shaped outline on 8½ in. by 11 in. white paper. Prepare twelve hearts in this manner. Print one of the kinds of hearts on each of the paper hearts. Place these around the room to use as signs during the

93

"Heart Beauty Shop" study of proverbs. If you have used the previous chapters, this can be a summary or review program.

Heart Beauty Shop

When virtue seems to be vanishing from our modern world, a visit to the Heart Beauty Shop of Proverbs reminds us

    1. that the problem is not new

    2. that the heart is the cause

Twelve kinds of hearts are described and prescribed for in this heart study.

Envious Heart. Be not thou envious against evil men, neither desire to be with them. For their *heart* studieth destruction, and their lips talk to mischief (Proverbs 24:1, 2).

Thinking Heart. For as he thinketh in his *heart,* so is he: Eat and drink, saith he to thee; but his *heart* is not with thee (Proverbs 23:7). . . . Pondereth the *heart* . . . render to every man according to his works (Proverbs 24:12).

Happy Heart. A merry *heart* doeth good like a medicine: but a broken spirit drieth the bones (Proverbs 17:22). A merry *heart* maketh a cheerful countenance: but by sorrow of the heart the spirit is broken (Proverbs 15:13).

Fretful Heart. Rejoice not when thine enemy falleth, and let not thine *heart* be glad when he stumbleth: . . . Fret not thyself because of evil men, neither be thou envious at the wicked (Proverbs 24:17, 19).

Hard Heart. Happy is the man that feareth alway: but he that hardeneth his *heart* shall fall into mischief (Proverbs 28:14).

Proud Heart. He that is of a proud *heart* stirreth up strife: but he that putteth his trust in the Lord shall be made fat. He that trusteth in his own *heart* is a fool: but whoso walketh wisely, he shall be delivered (Proverbs 28:25, 26).

Sick Heart. Hope deferred maketh the *heart* sick: but when the desire cometh, it is a tree of life (Proverbs 13:12).

Lustful Heart. Lust not after her beauty in thine *heart;* neither let her take thee with her eyelids (Proverbs 6:25).

Backslider Heart. The backslider in *heart* shall be filled with his own ways: and a good man shall be satisfied from himself (Proverbs 14:14).

Sound Heart. A sound *heart* is the life of the flesh: but envy the rottenness of the bones (Proverbs 14:30).

Understanding Heart. The *heart* of him that hath understanding seeketh knowledge: but the mouth of fools feedeth on foolishness (Proverbs 15:14).

Wicked Heart. Before we leave the "Heart Beauty Shop" of Proverbs, let us glance over the list of "six things doth the Lord hate: yea, seven are an abomination unto him: A proud look, a lying tongue, and hands that shed innocent blood, an *heart* that deviseth wicked imaginations, feet that be swift in running to mischief, a false witness that speaketh lies, and he that soweth discord among brethren" (Proverbs 6:16-19).

Let us remember this favorite summarizing proverb: Keep thy *heart* with all diligence; for out of it are the issues of life (Proverbs 4:23).

Dialogue

HAREM HOUSEHOLD

Setting: Garden area near House of the Women
Cast: Naamah and Persis

Both wives read the refrain.

PERSIS: Today the sun is hot and I am weary of life! See my gods on the high place yonder? They bring me no joy, though my king sometimes bows down before them to please me.

NAAMAH: Your gods are abomination, Persis! See how the sun gilds the temple. Surely my husband's Jehovah God is great! "He that walketh uprightly walketh surely" (Proverbs 10:9).

REFRAIN: "The eyes of the Lord are in every place, beholding the evil and the good" (Proverbs 15:3).

NAAMAH: Why are you sad, Persis? Remember "A merry heart maketh a cheerful countenance" (Proverbs 15:13). Smile and let your "merry heart doeth good like a medicine . . . a broken spirit drieth the bones" (Proverbs 17: 22).

PERSIS: Naamah, "by sorrow of the heart the spirit is broken" (15:13). I am sad because of Shiphrah. I envy her.

REFRAIN: "Envy thou not the oppressor, and choose none of his ways. . . . The wise shall inherit glory: but shame shall be the promotion of fools" (Proverbs 3:31, 35).

NAAMAH (*touching her lips*): "Whoso keepeth his mouth and his tongue keepeth his soul from troubles" (Proverbs 21: 23). My king knows "It is better to dwell in the wilderness, than with a contentious and an angry woman" (Proverbs 21:19).

PERSIS (*sighing*): "As vinegar to the teeth, and as smoke to the eyes . . ." (Proverbs 10:26), so I feel stifled here in the Hall of Women. My heart aches. My tears flow.

REFRAIN: "With her much fair speech she caused him to yield, with the flattering of her lips she forced him" (Proverbs 7:21). We honor our husband the king. His words are wise.

NAAMAH (*touching a gold earring*): "As an earring of gold, and an ornament of fine gold, so is a wise reprover upon an obedient ear" (Proverbs 25:12). You are my friend, Persis. How good it is to share my thoughts and moods with you this day!

PERSIS: Naamah, your words comfort me, and you are a wise woman. "He that walketh with wise men shall be wise: but a companion of fools shall be destroyed" (Proverbs 13:20).

REFRAIN: "A virtuous woman is a crown to her husband: but she that maketh ashamed is as rottenness in his bones" (Proverbs 12:4). We honor our husband the king. His words are wise.

NAAMAH (*shading eyes with one hand*): Ah, there is Shiphrah, strolling around the roof garden with her handmaidens.

PERSIS: "O how lofty are their eyes! and their eyelids are lifted up" (Proverbs 30:13).

NAAMAH: "Let thine eyes look right on [Persis], and let thine eyelids look straight before thee" (Proverbs 4:25).

REFRAIN: "Pride goeth before destruction, and an haughty spirit before a fall" (Proverbs 16:18). We honor our husband the king. His words are wise.

PERSIS (*sadly*): Today I feel old, Naamah. Look! See if you can find the white hair coming.

NAAMAH (*laughing*): "The hoary head is a crown of glory" (Proverbs 16:31). No, foolish Persis, you do not have white hair! Now my husband the king, he is growing old. "A wise man feareth, and departeth from evil" (Proverbs 14:16)

REFRAIN: "Give not thy strength unto women, nor thy ways to that which destroyeth kings" (Proverbs 31:3). We honor our husband the king. His words are wise.

PERSIS: See the proud Shiphrah! "There is a generation that are pure in their own eyes" (Proverbs 30:12). Yes, I must say I feel some sympathy for her, for she will soon have only her silver and gold for comfort.

NAAMAH: Yes, "A good name is rather to be chosen than great riches, and loving favour rather than silver and gold" (Proverbs 22:1). Your friendship to me means more than the wealth of this kingdom.

REFRAIN: "The house of the wicked shall be overthrown: but the tabernacle of the upright shall flourish. There is a way which seemeth right unto a man, but the end thereof are the ways of death" (Proverbs 14:11, 12). We honor our husband the king. His words are wise.

NAAMAH: I have lived at this court for a long time and I believe my husband the king when he says, "The highway of the upright is to depart from evil: he that keepeth his way preserveth his soul" (Proverbs 16:17).

PERSIS: He also says, "A violent man enticeth his neighbour, and leadeth him into the way that is not good" (Proverbs 16:29).

REFRAIN: "Fools make a mock at sin: but among the righteous there is favor" (Proverbs 14:9). "The wicked flee when no man pursueth: but the righteous are bold as a lion" (Proverbs 28:1). We honor our husband the king. His words are wise, and his wealth and power are known throughout the land.

Discussion

1. *Virtue.* Two Greek words used in the Scripture have been translated "virtue" in the English. One term *areté* denotes pure thoughts, godly action, moral goodness (2 Peter 1:5). This word is used also for modesty and purity in Philippians 4:8. The second word *dunamis* indicates power and strength (Mark 5:30; Luke 6:19)—the power Jesus had to heal disease.

Do you believe that pure thoughts and clean living are the basis of power and strength in our lives? Consider Proverbs 16:3 and 23:7.

2. *Four Idols.* When you think of idolatry, you probably think of ancient statues of gold or marble, and of Romans and Greeks bowing to Thor and Zeus, or Moses' brother Aaron who built the golden calf. Francis Bacon, English author and philosopher, suggests these four counterfeit deities that may intrude into our lives:

(a) *The Idol of the Tribe.* Going along with the crowd; ruled by fads and fashions; observing the respectable sin of silence when evil prevails and virtue vanishes.

(b) *The Idol of the Cave.* Allowing the home, its furnishings and personal comfort to take the place of God. Furniture cannot replace faith. Gadgets cannot come before God.

(c) *The Idol of the Marketplace.* Keep moneymaking in the marketplace. Do not commercialize your convictions. (Ideas from Chapter VII may be used in this discussion.)

(d) *The Idol of the Theater.* Mr. Bacon is not condemning the theater, but "hypocrisy"—playing a part. People who pretend to be better (or worse!) than they really are.

Keep yourself from such idols! (*Read 1 John 5:21.*)

3. Discuss the problem of wanting to be like another person you know rather than using Jesus as the model. Consider this thought: "She tried to be somebody, by trying to be like everybody, which makes her a nobody."

The Virtuous Woman

Who can find a virtuous woman? for her price is far above rubies.

The heart of her husband doth safely trust in her, so that he shall have no need of spoil. She will do him good and not evil all the days of her life.

She seeketh wool, and flax, and worketh willingly with her hands. She is like the merchants' ships; she bringeth her food from afar.

She riseth also while it is yet night, and giveth meat to her household, and a portion to her maidens. She considereth a field, and buyeth it: with the fruit of her hands she planteth a vineyard.

She girdeth her loins with strength, and strengtheneth her arms. She perceiveth that her merchandise is good: her candle goeth not out by night. She layeth her hands to the spindle, and her hands hold the distaff.

She stretcheth out her hand to the poor; yea, she reacheth forth her hands to the needy.

She is not afraid of the snow for her household: for all her household are clothed with scarlet. She maketh herself coverings of tapestry; her clothing is silk and purple.

Her husband is known in the gates, when he sitteth among the elders of the land.

She maketh fine linen, and selleth it; and delivereth girdles unto the merchant. Strength and honour are her clothing; and she shall rejoice in time to come.

She openeth her mouth with wisdom; and in her tongue is the law of kindness.

She looketh well to the ways of her household, and eateth not the bread of idleness. Her children arise up, and call her blessed; her husband also, and he praiseth her.

Many daughters have done virtuously, but thou excellest them all. Favour is deceitful, and beauty is vain: but a woman that feareth the Lord, she shall be praised. Give her of the fruit of her hands; and let her own works praise her in the gates.   *—Proverbs 31:10-31*

CHAPTER XIII

When You Seek Righteousness

**"He that followeth after righteousness
and mercy findeth life"
Proverbs 21:21**

THEME SONG: "Turn Your Eyes Upon Jesus"

SCRIPTURE: Proverbs 21:2, 12, 21; Ephesians 4:24-32

PRAYER: We come before Thee, heavenly Father, aware of Thy greatness and Thy love for us. We ask forgiveness of our sins, and guidance in seeking to live righteously. Help us each day to grow as Christians and to be worthy of Thy name. We praise Thee and thank Thee for all the good things in our lives. We especially thank Thee for Thy Son Jesus, in whose name we pray. Amen.

Preparation: Mimeograph a chart-calendar of the days of the month, possibly the month following presentation of this program. The inside pages of a church bulletin folder will be about the right size. If your church photo is on the cover, this can be used as a promotional pamphlet for community distribution.

Also mimeograph a list of thirty "righteous" proverbs, allowing space between each proverb for cutting the list into narrow strips. Fold the strips to fit the "day" spaces on the calendar, and tape a strip on each day of the month. Prepare a calendar for each member, who will open and read a verse every day for one month. You may prefer to make this a project for sharing with a shut-in "a proverb for every day."

Optional: Prepare copies of the "Proverbial Promises for Righteousness" as they appear on page 108, and distribute to members of the women's group.

The Influence of Women

Ever since the days of King Solomon, Biblical scholars have marveled at his wealth, his wisdom, and his women! He "loved many strange women" and when he was old, "his wives turned away his heart after other gods" (1 Kings 11:1-10). Do you wonder why such a wise man allowed his heart to be led away from God?

The influence of women, especially wives and mothers, is special and powerful. Tremendous pressure must have come from ladies in the king's harem! They wanted to worship their own gods and they brought a variety of cultures to the golden palace at Jerusalem. Poor old King Solomon had a vivid background of experiences, as well as a keen wit, as he phrased his proverbs. The alliteration of L's, as well as the thoughts, are beautiful in these verses:

> For the commandment is a lamp;
> and the law is light;
> and reproofs of instruction are the way of life:
> To keep thee from the evil woman,
> from the flattery of the tongue of a strange woman.
> —*Proverbs 6:23, 24*

Throughout the book of Proverbs two kinds of women have been contrasted: the strange woman like a deep ditch or narrow pit (Proverbs 22:14) and the virtuous woman (Proverbs 31:10-31). Even when a woman is not corrupt, Proverbs suggests that she can be contentious and fretful, so as to make the home unbearable. What a whimsical touch of humor this is: The attempt to restrain her is like trying to grasp the wind (Proverbs 27:16)!

A beautiful woman with no scruples is "as a jewel of gold in a swine's snout"—a fair woman without discretion (Proverbs 11:22). What an earthy comparison this is!

All these references to good and bad women merely show a woman's importance and influence in the lives of others, even in the ancient times of Solomon. Her place in life is so supreme that if she fails in her duty, civilization as a whole is a failure. The wisdom of woman builds her house, and the folly of woman plucks it down with her hands (Proverbs 14:1).

How ironical that the best things in life may be perverted to become the worst! Sex, love, marriage, home, even religion can become sinful rather than sacred when man and woman tamper with the rules for righteous living.

"A gracious woman retaineth honour" (Proverbs 11:16). The honor and respect she commands decides the kind of society. Pure and wholesome she leads men to purity, truth, and strength. Corrupt, proud, and false, she degrades a man to the level of an animal. He will be what she wants him to be. Her influence is important.

This is a divine arrangement for male-female relationships, planned by God when He created a companion for Adam. Slave or free, meek or aggressive, good or bad, a woman has a peculiar influence that makes or mars lives.

This fact is as true in the 1970's as it was in the golden days of Solomon's reign. Modern woman, in achieving certain freedoms, has destroyed in herself the qualities that make her beautiful and righteous: modesty, purity, chastity.

"If honor be your clothing, the suit will last a lifetime;

but if clothing be your honor, it will soon be worn thread-
bare" (Arnot).

How does a person acquire righteousness? Do you know
many people earnestly seeking righteousness? What does
"righteous" really mean?

The Wisdom of God

The predominant theme of Proverbs is the realism of
folly and the idealism of wisdom. Folly is historically pictured
as a wanton woman, and was observed by the author-king
when he looked through his window and beheld the miserable
and foolish young men. Wisdom, however, in many verses
becomes prophetic, as though glimpsed through the window
of the soul. Try this exercise: Use "Christ" everywhere that
the word wisdom appears in the Proverbs and notice the wonderful power of the verses. (Compare Proverbs 8:23-31 with
with John 1:1, 2; Colossians 2:3; 1 Corinthians 1:30.)

The wisdom of God is revealed in His creation, by sending
His Son, and in all His relationships with mankind through the
ages. Reading His holy Word, living by the principles found
there, will lead us into paths of righteousness—right living.

Psalms prepare the heart for meditation and worship in
the temple of the Lord; the proverbs prepare the feet for
walking in the marketplace. The language of the psalms is
lofty and poetic. The words of the proverbs are leveling and
pungent. They cut and gouge and make us feel that righteousness cannot be attained!

Our hearts yearn as we look for something that the book
of Proverbs cannot provide. Warnings, yes. Instructions, yes.
But as a person sinks deeper into the depths of sin, what hope
is there? Only Jesus has the answer. The personified wisdom
in the philosophical proverbs is not enough.

The eloquent Beatitude, "Blessed are the pure in heart:
for they shall see God" (Matthew 5:8) opens the door of

heaven to the pure in heart. It is a message of doom to those who have not attained righteousness. Jesus came "to seek and to save that which was lost" (Luke 19:10). This is the message of hope for all who feel that righteousness is out of reach.

The good news of the gospel message is found in the New Testament—the forgiveness of sins that comes when a life is given to Jesus, when all past mistakes are washed away and a new life begins.

A proverbial glimpse of hope is revealed in this verse: "The name of the Lord is a strong tower: the righteous runneth into it, and is safe" (Proverbs 18:10).

When we accumulate good deeds, think of them as our righteousness, and become proud of our goodness, we are indulging in a false kind of righteousness. We are trying to *earn* something. True righteousness, the kind that God requires, cannot be achieved by man. It does not come by effort, but by faith: "I count all things but loss for the excellency of the knowledge of Christ Jesus my Lord: . . . not having mine own righteousness, which is of the law, but that which is through the faith of Christ, the righteousness which is of God by faith" (Philippians 3:8, 9).

Does your righteousness consist only of satisfaction because of what you've done for the Lord? Proverbs 20:9 asks, "Who can say, I have made my heart clean, I am pure from my sin?" Proverbs 20:24 asks, "Man's goings are of the Lord; how can a man then understand his own way?"

When Jesus returned to His heavenly home, He left a Comforter (John 14:16) and a church (Ephesians 5:22-33) so that His followers would have guidance in the way of righteousness. The church is not composed of perfect people; it is a wonderful fellowship, however, of redeemed people who have turned to Christ for help. How discouraging it would be to seek to pattern our righteousness after another Christian! No, our eyes must be turned toward Jesus. We must try to grow into the full stature of His righteousness.

Do you remember how Jesus was criticized for associating with sinners? He replied that it is the sick people who need the physician (Luke 5:31).

In the Bible we find the history of man's failure to save himself, even when he does his best. His best is not good enough! The Bible also reveals God's plan, through the old and the new covenants, to redeem man from his sins. God's way is the best way!

This is an age of seeking and searching. People are restless, hungry for something beyond this temporal world. "I have immortal longings in me" (Shakespeare, *Antony and Cleopatra*). "As the hart panteth after the water brooks, so panteth my soul after thee, O God. My soul thirsteth for God, for the living God: when shall I come and appear before God?" (Psalm 42:1, 2). God has the peace a sinful, seeking world needs. God's love for us is not a love that exempts us from trials, but rather, a love that sees us through trials. His love is long-suffering and patient, as He gives the sinful seeker time to find His way.

How difficult it is even for Christians to understand God's grace—His love and concern for individuals. But we must share what we do understand with the searchers. "The fruit of the righteous is a tree of life; and he that winneth souls is wise" (Proverbs 11:30). How wise are you?

God's Love

What is knowledge worth when buried
    Like a jewel in the earth?
If we know God's love, this knowledge
    Must live in us—giving birth
To a love that feels for others,
    Looks upon them from God's side.
Lord, keep me close in that knowledge,
    Let me in Thy love abide.

                    —Adapted

Quotes for Discussion

1. "Human beings must be known to be loved; divine beings must be loved to be known." Do you agree?
2. Are roots necessary? "Morality without religion has no roots. It becomes a thing of custom, changeable, transient, and optional" (Henry Ward Beecher). Consider Proverbs 21:2.
3. "Religion is the best armor in the world, but the worst cloak" (John Newton). Does "cloak" mean hypocrisy?
4. Discuss the importance of persistence in the effort to live righteously. Consider Proverbs 24:16.
5. What can the women in your town do to promote "right" living, respect for authority, and honor among citizens? List specific projects, then do them!

Proverbial Promises for Righteousness

The hope of the righteous shall be gladness: but the expectation of the wicked shall perish. . . . The lips of the righteous know what is acceptable.
—Proverbs 10:28, 32

The righteous is delivered out of trouble, and the wicked cometh in his stead. . . . When it goeth well with the righteous, the city rejoiceth.
—Proverbs 11:8, 10

The desire of the righteous is only good. . . . The fruit of the righteous is a tree of life. . . . Behold, the righteous shall be recompensed in the earth.
—Proverbs 11:23, 30, 31

Righteousness exalteth a nation: but sin is a reproach to any people.   *—Proverbs 14:34*

In the house of the righteous is much treasure . . . The Lord is far from the wicked: but he heareth the prayer of the righteous.   *—Proverbs 15:6, 29*

Better is a little with righteousness than great revenues without right.   *—Proverbs 16:8*

He that followeth after righteousness and mercy findeth life, righteousness, and honour.   *—Proverbs 21:21*

For a just man falleth seven times, and riseth up again: but the wicked shall fall into mischief.
—Proverbs 24:16

Whoso walketh uprightly shall be saved: but he that is perverse in his ways shall fall at once.
—Proverbs 28:18

When the righteous are in authority, the people rejoice: but when the wicked beareth rule, the people mourn.   *—Proverbs 29:2*

The Christian Woman

A modern parable

Behold, there was a Christian woman who had lived in a worthy
manner lo these many years.

And as she considered all the good she had done, she let each
good deed, each kind word become part of a stone wall of
purity that began to close in upon her life of service.

She said, "I feel so safe and secure here with all this goodness
around me, I need not worry any more about evil in my life
or in the lives of others. I know all the methods to use and
all the right words to say; I will go no farther. I will rest here
until He comes."

And behold, there was a second Christian woman who also had
lived in a worthy manner lo these many years.

As she considered all the good she had done, the deeds appeared
to be a steep and sturdy flight of stairs, with the steps going
onward and upward, rising out of sight.

She said, "Lo, there is a marvelous vista from each step of this
high stairway. But there is still so much to learn, to see, to do.
I must keep climbing the stairs toward Him."

And behold, there was a third Christian woman who was new in
the field of Christian living.

She looked at other Christian women and saw the high stone wall
that kept some safe and secure and self-sufficient. She stood
on the bottom step of service and stared up the steep steps
toward Christian maturity.

She said, "The choice is mine. What manner of life will mine be?
Will I walk worthily of the Saviour who died for me?"

Index